Keep the Money Coming

A Step-by-Step Strategic Guide to Annual Fundraising

CHRISTINE GRAHAM

PINEAPPLE PRESS, INC.
SARASOTA, FLORIDA

Inquiries should be addressed to:

Pineapple Press, Inc.
P.O. Box 3889
Sarasota, Florida 34230

www.pineapplepress.com

Library of Congress Cataloging in Publication Data

Graham, Christine P., 1947–
Keep the money coming : a step-by-step strategic guide to annual fundraising / Christine Graham.— Rev. ed.
p. cm.
Includes bibliographical references.
ISBN 1-56164-227-4 (pbk. : alk. paper)
1. Fund raising—United States. 2. Nonprofit organizations—United States. I. Title.

HV41.9.U5 G72 2001
658.15'224—dc21

00-052437

10 9 8 7 6 5 4 3 2

Design by Millicent Hampton-Shepherd
Printed in the United States of America

TABLE OF CONTENTS

With great thanks to the hard-working, dedicated people I have met and collaborated with in so many diverse organizations, who helped me learn both the skills and the spirit of fundraising.

My special thanks to Catherine Cumpston, who first introduced me to fundraising, always with the emphasis on values and mission, and who taught me that paying attention to the thousand little details is the secret to overall success.

INTRODUCTION

Raising money is really not a mysterious skill. It is well within the ability of anyone who feels genuine concern for a group or project needing help. There is, though, real magic to the wonderful success of fundraising done effectively.

To raise money, you need four basic ingredients: common sense, organization, commitment and willingness to work. This book is offered as a form of technical assistance to augment those ingredients. It is a summary of the skills, ideas and techniques that have proven important to me time and again. None of these should supplant your understanding of your organization or your own good judgment if you've approached each issue with an open mind. Remember that people will give because of the organization, not just the fundraising techniques, and *you* are the expert on your organization.

Asking questions is the best method I've found for helping organizations develop their own most appropriate and successful fundraising plans. Many of the questions in this booklet could be answered quickly and in a word or two, but please take the opportunity to consider the underlying issues as well. The better you understand your people and your mission, the better you can provide for the future.

I also know from experience that organizations facing fundraising needs want to "hurry up and fix it." Everyone wants to get the problem solved and the fundraising out of the way fast. Don't allow yourselves to dismiss this effort as a short-term, uncomfortable assignment. Planned fundraising is a great way to build your organization, come to terms with difficulties, develop better staff and board cooperation, and strengthen your effort all around. Raising money will be just the first accomplishment of your fundraising effort. A healthy, successful organization will be your long-term acheivement.

Section One ■ Understanding Annual Funds

Your biggest area of expense each year is surely operations — the cost of staying in business. How do you spend that money? A little at a time, all year long. Be consistent. Raise it the same way, stay ahead, and you've got an annual fund.

1 ANNUAL FUNDS

To help you provide important services year after year, your donors must give year after year.

The foundation of your organization's healthy budget is the annual fund drive. The two keys to understanding the annual fund are: you raise the money every year, and it pays for expenses that recur every year.

If you need any money at all from contributions, an annual fund is the natural place to start. It allows great flexibility in planning and implementation. You can raise a little, or a lot. You can work on it year-round, or for a brief time. You can raise the money from a handful of "angels" or from hundreds of small givers. You can choose from scores of methods of fundraising, depending on your volunteers, your skills, your needs and your determination.

Always keep in mind these two key aspects of annual funds: the money pays for your operating expenses, and you can raise it every year.

Consider the impact of paying for your operating expenses. The real but hidden killer for organizations can be the ongoing expense of simply staying in business. Add to that the attraction, for volunteers and board members, of a highly publicized, popular capital drive or project fundraiser, and you can see the threats against raising your much-needed base of support.

There's plenty of charisma to raising money for a one-time, visible project or building. You can get grants for innovative ideas and projects, and seed money for new ventures. But underneath it all is your basic operation: salaries, office supplies, utilities, mileage, postage, printing. Although these are not galvanizing ideas for your donors, they are the guts of the organization that allow you to make everything else happen. You've got to pay for that first, and you've got to pay for it year after year. Let it slip and you'll be carrying the resultant deficit for years, along with failing morale, poor public relations and volunteer exhaustion. If the deficit alone doesn't threaten your survival, the accompanying burdens will.

With an annual drive, you sell your donors on your mission. You convince them that you, as an organization, are worthwhile. You are providing a valuable service. You deserve to thrive. And, like themselves, you have regular costs of living.

If you present your case with straightforward common sense, anyone can see that we all have operating expenses. That brings us to the true meaning of annual giving: To help you provide important services year after year, your donors must give year after year. To keep you running smoothly, they must give regularly.

The annual drive is the place to start. It is the only repeating fundraising effort that produces money to pay your operating costs.

If you present your donors with a strong mission, demonstration of continuing need, and a good plan for continuation of service, they will happily help you thrive. They don't need short-term charisma or flash-in-the-pan ventures if they are convinced that your mission is important and that you fulfill it well. Year after year, you build on the good arguments for support that you have presented in the past, and you build your donors' loyalty.

Charitable giving, as you will learn from observation, has many fascinating characteristics. For one, it is a habitual involvement. As discerning as donors may be, they tend to give to some of the same organizations year after year. It may be difficult to attract their gifts the first two or three years, but once you get past year three, the habit is set. If you are reliably consistent, they will be too.

Another characteristic is that donors tend to think of their contribution as an investment. Their dollars invest in your ability to fulfill your mission, so they will give once, and then they will give again next year to put more money into the cause. As in any venture, your success will encourage them to reinvest, again and again, to help you acheive more success.

As you learn about donors' thinking and decision-making processes, you can plan your annual campaign to encourage maximum giving. You'll learn the value of consistency, positive approach, communication, and most of all, gratitude.

The annual fund is the perfect place to master these fundraising techniques and to build your organization's capacity. But if you still are not convinced that an annual fund is the place to start your fundraising program, consider the bonuses it will bring you. Not only will you attract renewable gifts, but you can also use your annual drive to gain higher visibility in your community and the press, to attract energetic volunteers, to increase the number of donors and prospects willing to support your special drives, and to offer your staff the kind of stability they need in order to work to their greatest ability.

Eventually, particularly if you are successful now, you may look ahead to a more challenging financial goal, like a capital campaign or other big project. With a healthy annual fund within your operation, you'll be poised and ready with identified prospects, devoted donors, strong reputation, institutional knowledge and comfort with fundraising, an active board of directors and a sound operating budget. These factors will all make higher goals more readily acheivable when the time is right and the need is there.

But remember, the annual drive is the place to start. It is the only repeating fundraising effort that produces money to pay your operating costs. If you need to raise money for operations, the annual drive is the single approach that will offer you the greatest diversity of fundraising methods and the widest range of auxiliary impacts. It is the one approach that best prepares your organization for the future, through strong finances and increased capability.

2 WHY PEOPLE GIVE

Promises of big chunks of money will always be beckoning your staff and board. Grants, bequests and big-ticket events all have the allure of winning the lottery and often offer windfalls for apparently little effort. If one of them actually comes your way, naturally you won't refuse it; but for consistent, year-after-year reliability, those sources are dangerously attractive. They encourage you to rely on fate, procrastinate and avoid responsibility; even when they work out, they do nothing to build the organization's future.

In fact, few windfalls come without long hard work behind the scenes. Most of that work will take far longer than one year, making the eventual gift inappropriate for reliable annual funding. And most of the windfalls occur only once, again cutting away at the annual funding idea. No one would stop you from hoping for a windfall or from spending a portion of your time working on long-term gifts. But be realistic. Look for the repeating smaller gifts annually. With luck, your hard work there will earn you the windfalls later. Most of the wild stories you read about surprise multimillion-dollar bequests come from people who spent many years quietly admiring an organization's work and success. If you are lucky enough to get one, establish or augment your endowment, and the income will help your annual budget. But be realistic!

Your job is beguilingly simple: find those people and ask them for money.

Your best source of funding, for annual drives and nearly any other kind of fundraising, will be people: individuals who appreciate your organization. Regardless of your particular situation, old or new, radical or conservative, quiet or flashy, there are people who will relate to your organization and want to help you.

Your job is simple: find those people and ask them for money.

Not so simple, you say? Well, this job *would* be simple if we were not all human beings with worries, fears of failure, egos and shyness, a tendency to procrastinate and a thousand other things to do. If you are going to organize a fundraising drive for your organization, you should accept the fact that you, and all your volunteers, are human. Half your job will be to learn how to raise money and the other half will be to get yourselves to do it.

You will do well in this business if you start out believing the best of people. After you've been fundraising for a while, it will be almost impossible to believe anything else. The extraordinary generosity that will flow from people after you've presented them with a strong cause is enough to warm any heart.

People have a remarkable capacity for creating change and for supporting others. Faced with the right reason, donors will not only give money but will become your best spokespeople too. As donors give more, they become more adamant, dedicated, and outspoken. As long as you hold up your end of the bargain, and run a healthy organization that is making a difference, your donors will be faithful and increasingly supportive. Your best prospects for the future are your donors today.

You may think this sounds fine for other organizations, but that yours is a bit too small, too narrow, too focused or too controversial to attract real dedication. That is never the case. If there is one thing shared by all people, it is their capacity for diversity. There are donors out there for your cause, provided you express it eloquently and with commitment.

Focus on your mission: your organization's purpose for existence. This is the reason you raise money, and this is the real reason people give you money.

One of the great concerns you have may be the financial ability of your members and friends. Many human service organizations, particularly, worry that their donors simply do not have the money to support them in a big way. For you, it is important to remember that the most generous donors in the United States are those at the lower income levels. While Americans give away an average 2.5% of their income, those who earn just $10,000 to $20,000 a year give 3.2%. People earning between $50,000 and $75,000 give 1.8%, and those earning over $100,000 give 2.9%. Granted, 2.9% of $100,000 is more than 3.2% of $10,000, but there are plenty of donor prospects at the lower levels, and the strength of their support will give you the consistency you need.

The best way to surmount your own human frailities is to focus on your mission: your organization's purpose for existence. This is the reason you will raise money, and this is the real reason people will give you money. We call it *charitable intent*, and it is a stronger and more reliable motivator than peer pressure, tax incentives, social status, a feeling of involvement, insecurity, obtaining favors or increasing prestige. Many of those other motivators work, but the only one that truly lasts, and the only one that will distinguish you from all the other nonprofits out there, is your mission.

You need a strong, accurate statement for annual fundraising, but you also need it for wise decision making and day-to-day effectiveness. Reviewing, revamping and rewriting the statement is not a quick job, but it need not bring all work to a halt. It is crucial to all your activities. This is a great job for board/staff cooperation and can be done by yourselves or with a facilitator. Once you've identified your mission as the place to start, you have begun working on building your annual fund.

3 ARE YOU READY?

You must have demonstrated financial needs to raise funds. On the other hand, dire financial disaster is not an attractive motivator for donors either.

The annual fund should meet your specific, identified needs, not force your organization to fit a mold. It can be as big or small, as ambitious or modest, as easy or challenging as you want to make it. Also, it will be as successful as you make it. You are in control. Make it work for you.

All you really need to get started are a strong organization and a need for money.

A strong organization is one that has a clearly defined mission, a reason to operate, a plan for action, goals and plans. This is not as simple as it sounds! Many an organization discovers, to its horror, that it is not really focused on a purpose; too often this discovery occurs when the staff and board begin to try to raise money. They can't agree on the description of the organization and its work.

If you find that your mission is unclear or that you are operating without real understanding of community needs, take a break from your fundraising planning and do some serious work on both needs assessment and organizational planning. If your staff and board cannot make a strong case for support, in words or in writing, no donor will be convinced. No one wants to give money to a group that doesn't know what it is doing, or that cannot defend each goal it sets and each dollar it spends.

Assessing your mission is not a one-time job; like annual fundraising, you should do it regularly. Each member of your board and staff should be able to describe the mission clearly and succinctly. You must regularly review community needs and set goals to meet those needs in terms of your organization's purposes. Don't be afraid of challenges, and don't expect to be 100% successful in meeting your goals before you ask for money. It's the need, and understanding of it, that makes you ready to do serious planning and fundraising. While high standards are admirable, no one can expect you to wait till you are perfect before you ask for money.

In fact, you must have demonstrated financial needs to raise funds. There's so much competition these days that the group raising money to shore up its Rainy Day Fund will have a hard time sounding needy. On the other hand, dire financial disaster is not an attractive motivator for donors either. People really prefer to back a winner.

The time to raise funds is when support is needed for a projected budget. The best situation is to plan for a fund drive in advance of the need. If you can do this, you are lucky. In fundraising, you always want to find the balance between disaster and surplus: to show that you truly need support to continue good operations, not to bail you out.

You will be faced continually with this search for a reasonable balance in fundraising. You have to set goals that challenge but don't devastate you; assign tasks that stretch abilities but don't discourage your volunteers; plan in advance but don't plan to the point of losing flexibility; and ask donors to give more but don't overtax their goodwill.

To ascertain your readiness for an annual drive, answer these two initial questions:

- Can we state our mission clearly?
- Can we demonstrate need?

If you need work on either of these questions, or have the wisdom to check your readiness, work with staff and/or board to implement the exercises suggested below.

When you have satisfied yourselves on these basic points, you will be ready to move ahead. These clarifying points will help you all along also. They are touchstones. See Figure 1 on the next page for questions to ask yourselves for determining your readiness for annual fundraising.

These questions are designed to help you pinpoint the areas where you are ready and where you are not. Take "no" answers as your directions for beginning work, not as discouragement. Go through these questions with common sense, with several key people who know your group well, and you can soon do adequate preparatory work for a strong fund drive. Ignoring these issues early will give you a mistaken sense of security, and later you will find yourselves in trouble.

There is no such thing as a nonprofit organization that cannot raise funds. But there are far too many groups that take the plunge without being adequately prepared. The ones who succeed are the ones who take the time to prepare. You can be one of those!

Figure 1: Determining Readiness

On basic organization:

- Are we a 501 (c)(3) organization?
- Are we in operation, or do we have a start-up plan?
- Do we have a long-range plan, strategic plan, and fundraising plan?

On financial matters:

- Is our budget lean, without destroying effectiveness?
- Do we operate in a responsible, ethical and cost-efficient manner?
- Are our salaries fair and competitive?
- Do we maintain good bookkeeping practices?
- Do we report regularly to our board and/or members in a manner they can understand?

On mission and goals:

- Do we have a clearly stated, updated mission?
- Do we plan for the future and learn from the past?
- Do we try to understand the people we serve and their needs?
- Do we issue an annual report or communicate our progress effectively in another way?
- Do we evaluate our progress with an open mind to improvements and refinements, including the possibility of retiring programs?

On people: board, staff and volunteers:

- Do we regularly educate our board and volunteers about our operations and their roles?
- Is the board involved in fundraising?
- Is the whole organization committed to the importance of fundraising?
- Do we have dedicated volunteers, in sufficient numbers?
- Do we have responsible and humane personnel practices, and do we treat our volunteers and board members equally well?
- Do we show appreciation?

On public relations:

- Does our community know us and what we do?
- Do we project a strong and ethical image?
- Are we respected for providing good service?
- Does our public relations effort continually attract new supporters?
- Do we understand the ways in which public relations is an integral part of funding our operation?
- Is the community prepared to support us?
- Have we considered the impact our fundraising may have on our image?
- Have we cooperated with our peer groups in establishing plans?

On running the fund drive:

- Have we made fundraising a priority?
- Have we made staff time to work on the campaign?
- Do we have board members and volunteers who will work on the campaign?
- If we don't have fundraising experience, have we obtained technical assistance?
- Are we methodically approaching establishment of prospect lists, plans, goals and deadlines?
- Do we have our record-keeping and thanking systems set up?
- Have we budgeted for fundraising costs?

Be realistic: Fundraising takes time! Start at the beginning and develop a systematic approach. Pace yourself. You'll build strengths that will accumulate, year after year.

4 GOALS AND NEEDS

If you have a broad overview of your organization, you know that fundraising is a means to an end. It is just a tool for accomplishing the goals you set for your organization. As important as money is, it does not come first in your planning. Therefore, it may help you to distinguish between program needs and goals, and fundraising needs and goals. This book covers fundraising, with an insistence on strong

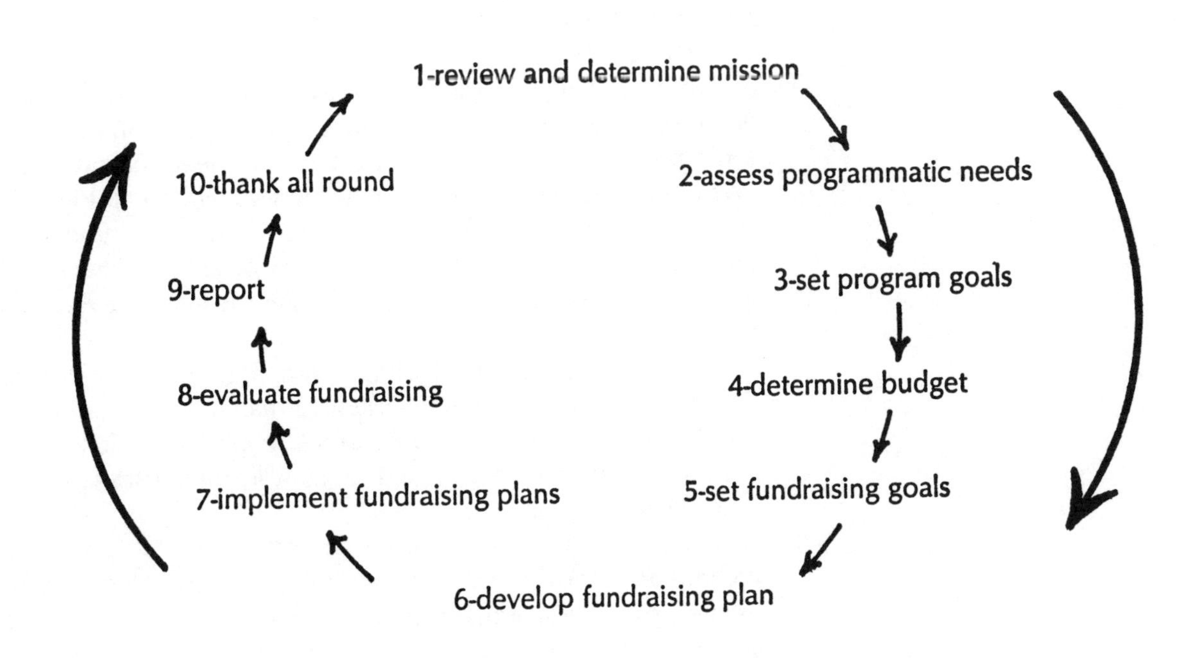

programmatic planning first. Try to think of your organization's efforts in a chronological, cyclical pattern:

Beside giving you a clear understanding of the order of events, this cycle helps clarify the relationship between program needs and goals, and those of fundraising. Our consideration starts midcycle, with setting fundraising goals. Your dollar goal will determine much of the structure and spirit of your fundraising operation, so consider it carefully. Start with three key questions:

- How much do you need to raise?
- How much *can* you raise?
- How do you reconcile these two, and set the goal?

HOW MUCH DO YOU NEED?

All things being equal, you should raise enough money annually to close the gap between yearly income and expense. There may be some reasons why you cannot do this right away, or why you may attempt to raise a bit more, but first let's consider that gap, and how to determine its size.

Before you start fundraising plans, you need a budget for overall operations. Work on the budget. Make sure your expense projections provide adequately to meet program goals; not only is that your primary assignment, but it will be increasingly difficult to raise money in the future if you don't do your job well now. With falsely modest budget projections, you'll never be able to meet programmatic goals and keep your organization intact.

In addition to sufficient budgeting for program needs, make sure you have budgeted for fundraising costs. At the very least, you'll need paper and postage, and coffee and cookies for your volunteers. Eventually you may need to spend much more than that. Fundraising is not free. Like any business, you'll have to spend some money to make money. Keep your costs modest, within the context of your overall budget, but do include them.

Get your budget approved by the board after they've read it over and discussed it. Your board's support is crucial to an annual fund, and those people are your best supporters. You need their support, and, to give it, the board needs to feel comfortable with the budget. Take time on this. Imagine the outcome of a gift solicitation, should your board member struggle to defend the budget, or answer probing questions with a blank look. Think of your budget as the first of several fundraising tools.

The second part of budgeting is preparation of the income projection. Neglecting this leads to "intuitive management," a nice term that translates to scrambling, panic and last-minute deficits. It is just as important to know where your money will come from as to know what you will spend it on.

Before you even think about adding an annual fund goal to your income projection, look at all your other sources of income: fees, sales, assured grants, government funds, endowment income, regular in-kind support, and earned income. At this point you should only include income you are guaranteed: if you must ask for it, if someone else holds the purse strings, or if it will require any form of solicitation at all, do not include it.

All the "iffy" funds, those that you will have to raise through new efforts throughout the year, should be listed as gifts and contributions. One category of gifts and contributions is the annual fund. There may be others, such as special project funds, capital gifts, grants and bequests. Keep these newly solicited funds separate from guaranteed income in your budget, primarily to remind you that work is involved in obtaining the money, and that someone else's choices will determine if you will get the funds. If those "guaranteed" funds fall through, you'll have to replace them with even more gifts and contributions.

You can do quick simple arithmetic to find the difference between projected expense and projected income. That difference is your "gap": the dollars that stand between need and available funds. That difference is also, in most circumstances, your annual fund goal. After you answer the next two questions, and perhaps after you adjust the budgets, you'll be ready to approve it.

HOW MUCH CAN YOU RAISE?

Unfortunately, the formulas to determine the amount you CAN raise are not so easily obtained. With this question you begin to get into the more interesting parts of fundraising: the intangible, psychological, motivational parts of the job.

Begin by considering the intangibles issues, and ask yourselves some "perception questions":

How high a priority is our mission, in this community?

- How healthy is the economy? How are retail sales? What is the unemployment rate today?
- Is this an area where charitable giving is accepted? common? unfamiliar?
- How hard will our board members work?
- Do our board members have money themselves, and/or contacts with other good prospects?
- Are we competing with similar organizations that have terrific fundraising histories?
- Are there any political problems surrounding our mission?
- Are we perceived as an organization that should be able to thrive without contributions?

If you understand the forces that will be working against you, you can design a stronger campaign.

Your assignment at this point is to determine which issues of public perception will have an impact on your ability to raise funds. You may be offended by this exercise. You may feel that your organization needs and deserves support so much that the intangibles don't matter. Still, you have to be realistic. You are the one who will count the dollars at the end of this fund drive, and ignoring the intangibles now will curtail your ability to tackle weak areas and raise maximum dollars.

You may just feel aggressively determined to get the funds you need. You will show the community what it should do! That level of determination is a great asset, and you mustn't lose your commitment now. But remember, if you understand the forces that will be working against you, you can design a stronger campaign.

As you can begin to see, this is an issue of balance. Simply setting your goal at the level of financial need may be too challenging and wear out your volunteers. You need them for the long haul, just like you need a healthy, growing annual fund for the long haul. In some rare cases, setting the goal at the level of need may not make the most of your volunteers and community sentiment on your behalf. In those cases, setting your goal too low can have a depressing effect for many years to come.

If you were conducting a capital campaign, you might conduct a feasibility study to get the answers to your questions. With an annual fund, these questions must be asked repeatedly, and you must be flexible enough to adapt your annual efforts to the changing fundraising scene.

When you first start out, the questions regarding competition will be key in determining the amount you can hope to raise. Over time, those questions will become less important and your willingness to work hard will become increasingly important. Use your history to your advantage, and start building that history now. Every acheivement in this year's campaign makes next year's effort better. It also helps contribute to your donors' giving habits, which you need to encourage.

Take your "gap" number, the amount between income and expense, and test it against the answers to your perception questions. Allow yourselves to react emotionally to the answers in terms of that number. For instance, if you have a budget of $267,000 and can project assured income of $235,000, you would test an imaginary goal of $32,000 by asking:

How high a priority is our mission, in this community?

Do people in our community feel we answer a real need? Is it worth $32,000 to them? Does that seem like too much money for this problem? If we don't do this, will it cost them more to answer the need elsewhere? Are we a luxury? Will our community pay $32,000 for a luxury?

How healthy is the economy? How are retail sales? What is the unemployment rate today?

Is there enough disposable income here to provide $32,000? Are people working, and are they making enough money to be spending on necessities? luxuries? comforts? Where do we fall in that list?

Is this an area where charitable giving is accepted?

Can we just raise money, or do we have to start with raising consciousness? Are there "angels" out there? Do people have habits of giving, and if so, at what level? Do they think of contributions as $5 door-to-door gifts, or $100 checks written monthly to a wide variety of charities?

In doing this exercise you will come to understand the range of challenges you face. You may find that the amount you CAN raise will have to be smaller than your "gap number." The younger your organization, and your fundraising operation, the more important it is to set an achieveable goal. Once you've had a long, successful history, you can take a chance on running short; in the beginning, people need to see you meet the goal in order to believe you are a serious effort. That has an impact on next year. After considering the psychology of your goal, you may have to go back to the budget and make it tighter this year.

Perhaps you'll find that this promises to be a good year, and you have the capability to raise more than you absolutely need. This wonderful experience occurs for a variety of reasons: if you have just completed a major, successful campaign, your donors may be in the habit of giving more and you'd like to take advantage of that habit. Some heavy competition from peer organizations may have just let up. You may have gotten some excellent, high-visibility press. You may have some new board members who are experienced, proven fundraisers. Whatever the reason, appreciate it and take advantage of the opportunity to raise your expectations. Depending upon the percentage of surplus, you may pay off debts, add to endowment, establish a revolving fund for tight times or extraordinary need, or simply carry over cash to the next year. Whatever you do, use it as an opportunity to set a new standard, and don't allow the annual fund to fall back in subsequent years.

SETTING THE GOAL

You might think that the goal for your annual fund is just a dollar amount that represents what you should raise to meet your needs. Actually, that is the barest beginning. In fact, your goal is a primary motivator, and it is much more valuable to you as an image and pacer than it is as representation of money in the bank. A goal is not a number, it's a challenge.

Your goal is a primary motivator, and it is much more valuable to you as an image and pacer than it is as representation of money in the bank. A goal is not a number, it's a challenge.

So here we are, back at the issue of balance. Your goal must challenge you, or you will not meet it! Believe it or not, keeping the goal low will not provide sufficient motivation for your reluctant fundraisers. They will not respond to your kind consideration by working quickly toward meeting a modest goal. They will simply work less than they'd planned, and you'll risk falling short of goal.

On the other hand, if you set the goal too high, they will be discouraged before they even get started, and they'll do less than they'd planned. You'll risk shortfall.

What you must find is the magic number that will cheer them on, make them work just a little harder than they'd imagined they would, and give them the wonderful, exhilarating feeling of success when they are done.

If you've been in the business a long time, and you've been running a strong annual fund for years, you may be able to set your goal by adding a percentage to last year's goal or total. That's the easy way. But remember, even in your predictable situation the goal should be carefully considered. There may be years when the percentage add-on could be a killer, like the first year of another major campaign. There may be other years when you could ratchet the goal higher than usual and encourage a one-time stretch that will take the annual fund to new, consistantly higher levels.

But let's assume that you are either new to the annual fund business or haven't got a reliable history of successful campaigns. You've done the first two exercises, and you have an idea of the amount you need to raise and the amount you may be able to raise. Only three conclusions are possible:

Need = Ability
Need > Ability
Need < Ability

Need = Ability

You have arrived at the lucky equation, and can set your goal at precisely your "gap" number. You will proceed immediately to the next assignment: going public. Before you feel too smug about this good fortune, remember that arriving at the lucky conclusion too many years in a row means you have not been tough enough in asking the Perception Questions. You may be letting yourselves off easy, and in doing so, belittling the ability of your organization to improve and grow.

Need > Ability

At least you have a lot of company here. Need is almost always greater than the ability to raise funds in the early years of an annual fund. You may actually have arrived at the decision to conduct an annual appeal due to budget problems, so this imbalance is probably no surprise.

You must adjust your budget to make the "gap number" approximate the amount you can raise, or rethink the amount you can raise. This is not an easy exercise, but if you have answered the Perception Questions honestly and thoroughly, your only option will be to adjust the budget down. Don't just hope for the best and go with a budget that you can't meet, even with a successful annual fund. Next year you'll pay a terrible price for that choice. Remember that even in annual fundraising, you are in it for the long haul. You will want this year to prepare the ground for a better fund next year.

Your first options for budget squeezing should be those things that will not impose on basic services and not interfere with your fundraising efforts. You do not want to tie your hands behind your backs. Consider cutbacks on supplies, impose monitoring of utilities, phones, and so on, select less-expensive printed materials, forego any luxuries, eliminate any social costs related to board meetings, and review all your budget items for belt-tightening but not severe cuts. If the gap still remains, you should reassess your fees: when was the last time you raised them, and are they competitive? Can people pay more? Will they? If there still is a big difference between projected income and projected expenses, you may have more than a cursory cut-back situation. Involve the board and the staff, and be realistic.

Remember that donated dollars do not spring surprisingly from the earth. You will work hard for each and every one. So you must not casually increase your annual fund goal simply to avoid dealing with very real budget problems. If the simple suggestions here don't do the trick, your board has to take a hard look at costs, services and programmatic goals. When the "gap" number is enormous, the possibility of raising it is small, and the situation has been this way for some time, look at serious issues of organizational viability, collaboration, merger and cut-backs in both costs and program. Remember that nothing is forever. Don't postpone the inevitable. Control the outcome by staying in touch with reality.

Need < Ability

This may be a once-in-a-lifetime occasion. Use your ability to raise more than you currently need to make identified long-term improvements in the organization. Don't lower your goal and take it easy for a year. You'll lose momentum and your community standing as a prime fundraiser, and some of your loyal donors will switch to more needy groups.

Setting a challenging goal is important for your workers and your sense of progress. You should take advantage of the ability to raise as much as you can and keep the spirit high.

If you are lucky enough to discover that you CAN raise more than the "gap number," use that advantage to plan for a healthy future. If you have a well-constructed strategic plan, you will easily see what choices can be made. Without a strategic plan, you might consider not spending endowment income this year, and instead reinvesting it. That way you'll be building a better Rainy Day Fund without imposing on the good argument of your need to raise funds for operations. (If you find yourselves in this situation and don't have a strategic plan, devote time to creating one now.)

If you think this may be a one-time occurrence, consider a special expenditure within your plan which can be funded with the overflow. Select something greatly needed, and something that will reduce operating costs in the future. Every organization has such wish-list items. It is important to select something that will augment regular operations, since this is, after all, the annual fund, and it is important to remember it funds operations. Look, too, for something that frees staff time, allows further training of staff and board, or updates the operation; greater efficiency and skill is an investment that will pay off in future years. This may be the opportunity to computerize or to update software, to prepare new outreach materials, to do community education, or fund start-up costs for a newsletter.

Unless you are secure in knowing you can raise more than you need every year, do not use the excess funds to raise salaries or add programs. Annual gift increases are very dangerous sources of funding for budget increases that will lead to subsequent, growing need year after year.

Perhaps there will be some unusual circumstances that make you hesitate, for good reason, about adapting your budget to the ability to raise more this year. But generally, setting a challenging goal is important for your workers and your sense of progress. You should take advantage of the ability to raise as much as you can and keep the spirit high.

Document add-ons that were funded through surpluses, and make certain all these circumstances are reviewed next year when the new goal is set. As wonderful as this opportunity is, you must not allow it to prepare you for failure or disappointment next year.

GOING PUBLIC

Even with all this careful internal planning, your volunteers may gasp at the goal. You know what you can raise, and you know what kind of a figure will get public acceptance. Your board members and solicitors, faced with raising the money, may gasp at any amount. You can make it palatable as well as challenging.

Remember that, within your income projections, there are many reliable sources: long-term pledges that are certain to come in, those in-kind gifts that must be solicited but are traditionally donated, any other gifts or contributions you expect with assurance. All these expected gifts may form a subtotal of "sure things" within your gifts and contributions category.

You can take the initial action and gather those gifts, through staff solicitation, and then do one of two things: subtract the subtotal from your total goal, setting a public goal for the actual new dollars you must raise, or announce the total goal along with the subtotal as "kick-off" funds to show some immediate progress. This is a choice for you to make based on your assessment of the psychological impact on your volunteers and your community.

Will the community be offended by a higher goal?

- Will the higher goal act as a challenge, or will it discourage our donors and volunteers?
- Will the fact that we can already declare some of the funds "raised" dilute the urgency of our appeal? Will the smaller goal seem so modest that it disappears compared with other community goals?
- What size gifts are you going to ask for first?

You can make these judgments based on the overall economy in your area, the types of volunteers you have, the goals and fundraising done by other groups in your area, and the kind of service you offer.

For instance, suppose you are a grass-roots group in a low-income area. Your average donors give $15 each, and you can count on $43,000 in assured gifts. Announcing a $75,000 goal may discourage your volunteers before they even get started. But by subtracting the $43,000 in assured gifts at the start, you may be able to announce a $32,000 goal for new gifts that seems challenging but manageable.

On the other hand, if your board is prepared to go out and ask for twenty-five $1,000 gifts before they begin the real grass-roots appeal, you may need to announce the higher goal to give them the back-up they need. It would be difficult to defend all those thousand dollar solicitations if only $32,000 was needed in total.

Working through your goal-setting exercise may seem complicated to you, and some of it is. But the end result should be simple: a goal that you know you can acheive if everyone works hard. When you announce the goal, it should be straightforward, clearly understood by all, and should demonstrate your ability to meet the budget for the year. A forthright goal, based on honest analysis, will be accepted. Simplicity and success are the natural results of careful planning. That's the next step.

5 PLANNING YOUR CAMPAIGN

If you have had trouble getting started with an annual fund in the past, or if you are feeling panicky about it now, chances are you haven't had a plan. If there's a single factor in any successful fundraising campaign — one that reaches goal without burning out staff and volunteers — it is a strong plan. Make sure you allow time and concentration to do this right.

ESSENTIAL CONCEPTS

Start Early

The right time to begin planning your annual campaign is the month before your fiscal year starts; if you are truly inundated with year-end efforts, you can compromise and plan during the first month of the fiscal year. Don't postpone it any longer, or you will lose fundraising time.

You will certainly want to conduct specific fund efforts in times proven best for donor response, such as mid-fall for a mail appeal. But within those plans, your fundraising calendar will have to coincide with your fiscal year in order to assure adequate fundraising to meet budget needs. Your donors will plan and respond on a calendar-year basis, but you can accomodate that, particularly by scheduling several opportunities for giving. Never wait till January to conduct fundraising for an organization with a July 1- June 30 fiscal year!

Allow enough time for thoughtful planning; time is never as long at the end of a fund year as it is at the beginning. Lost time can never be regained! Only by starting early can you consider the full range of profitable fundraising ideas suitable for your group.

Include staff and volunteers at the early stages

You need widespread commitment to your fundraising projects in order to get enough workers and attract enough donors. The only way to assure that kind of shared responsibility is through early involvement.

Some highly organized people have a hard time learning to involve many people in planning because the democratic process tends to be slow, but it is well worth the effort. Not only will you get more commitment, but you will find that your quiet dedicated workers can generate some wonderful ideas too! No one knows better what fundraising efforts will work than the friends and peers of your prospects. Listen to them. Pay attention, and question your own reliance on "tried-and-true" methods.

Diversify your efforts

Select a variety of methods to assure success and provide yourselves with back-up ideas. You need to protect yourselves from all the unforeseen, anxiety-producing events that can attack your campaign: rain on your carnival, bad press the day before the major mail piece goes out, unexpected staff changes mid-year, the loss of a top donor. You simply cannot afford to build an annual appeal based on one event, one donor who gives 70% of the goal, or any other single source.

Always use fund-raising success as a tool for planning your next expansion, and the time it buys you as opportunity for experimentation.

Many organizations fall accidently into relying on one source. For some, exhaustion from several years of tough fundraising with insufficient returns has weakened the effort and spirit so that a single major gift is like a life raft. The last thing staff and volunteers want to do is settle down to developing new sources: they want to relax and enjoy the comfort of success. But that is precisely the time to develop new sources: when you are riding high, and volunteers are happy and energized by success.

When you begin to rely too heavily on one or two donors, or on a special event that takes the community by storm, time slips by fast. You become extremely vulnerable and may even jeopardize that single source by behaving like a dependent child. Be careful. Always use fundraising success as a tool for planning your next expansion, and the time it buys you as opportunity for experimentation.

Stagger your efforts over a period of time

Annual fundraising is defined as raising money for one year's operations, not necessarily fundraising that lasts for one year. While you do not have to spread your annual fundraising campaign over an entire year, and in fact may choose not to in order to allow resting time, you will give yourselves far more opportunities to complete manageable tasks if you use the maximum time available.

Unless yours is an unusual group, you probably have some board members and volunteers who are superior fundraisers, and others who are not. To make the best use of the good ones, without wearing them out, you should spread out your efforts.

The community can accept your ambitious fundraising goals more easily if your solicitations, direct mail, events, and other methods are spread over time. In fact, your dedicated donors will probably contribute in several different ways if you approach them at different times.

Most donors respond to a mail appeal by consulting their checkbook. While you may be asking for an "annual gift" to help pay your annually recurring costs, your average donor is giving from his or her monthly discretionary funds, the amount "left over" after monthly bills are paid. If you could count on donors to determine their cumulative 12-month ability and commitment to support your yearly needs, one fund drive per year would be fine. But most people spend money, and give it away, in the same time frame that they earn it; therefore you can receive several smaller gifts from each donor which will add up to true "annual" support.

If you spread your efforts over time, a modest donor can often afford a $35 check in response to a mail appeal, plus a $25 ticket to a benefit dinner, plus $15 for raffle tickets, plus $25 for a special needs phone appeal. That $35 donor is really a $100 donor over the course of a year. If you'd asked for the $100 up front, he or she might have thought you were crazy.

Go for major gifts early in the year

Safety comes first in any annual fund. Even if you have admirable secondary goals such as increasing volunteer involvement, attracting new prospects, establishing strong board commitment, and creating a diverse fundraising plan, you must make meeting the goal your highest priority.

You must not squander any efforts on small dollar fundraising until you have given your best supporters a chance to give to the maximum. Start your fundraising year with personal solicitation of proven donors and your most promising prospects. Ask for true "annual support": a gift that will make a dent in your operating budget. Never allow a major donor to slip into your mail solicitation group without serious personal attention.

The days of black-tie benefits paying all the bills are over. You need to reach out to all parts of your community, to every person who may be committed to your cause, and give each one an opportunity to work and to give at his or her own personal level of ability.

Not only do you get a healthy start on your fund by soliciting major gifts first, but you give yourselves a gauge for determining the sort of fund year you may have. If the economy is tight, and major donors disappoint you, you still have time to augment other efforts. You also have time later in the year to go back to those same people and try again. If things go beautifully in the first month of solicitation, perhaps you can adjust a later effort to fund a much-needed special project or plan for a cash reserve that will take pressure off operations later. You might postpone a labor-intensive event, or reduce expectations (and, therefore, work) on another.

Most importantly, by starting with the major donors, you assure yourselves of retaining their support at high levels. Anyone who has lost a $1000 cash prospect because "I already bought a $100 benefit ticket" knows that first things must come first. Get the unrestricted gifts before plunging into special events. *Link your fundraising schedule to your spending.*

From a purely practical aspect, soliciting major gifts first gives you the influx of cash that you need to operate. If you wait till ten months into the fiscal year to bring in gifts, you may suffer serious cash flow problems despite the fact that you are carefully following a winning plan.

If you do all your fundraising in advance of need, this may not be a concern, but nearly all nonprofits use current fundraising dollars, at least in part, for current operations. Pace your fundraising and your spending so you do not have to make unnecessary compromises in program based on temporary cash flow problems.

Involve as many different types of people as you can

Fundraising should be an inclusionary activity. The days of black-tie benefits paying all the bills are over. You need to reach out to all parts of your community, to every person who may be committed to your cause, and give each one an opportunity to work and to give at his or her own personal level of ability. Professional volunteers are great, but few exist anymore due to dual-income and single-parent families. When someone offers a few hours a week, a Saturday morning once a month, you grab it, and gratefully! "Angel" patrons are still around, but you may not have one. You can raise the equivalent of that big dollar gift through many small gifts, with good grassroots efforts. More work, perhaps, but it can be done. You need every person committed to your cause, working and giving.

Link your fundraising schedule to your spending.

You also need many different types of people involved in your work, because they attract their friends to the effort. You can build your numbers, and attract new prospects, by spreading your efforts. Today, people's interests change more rapidly and the range of nonprofits is broader than 20-30 years ago. If you do not bring in new prospects in significant numbers, your donor base can dissolve as much as 30% per year — not because you are doing a bad job in providing good service, running important programs, and meeting your mission, but because you are not finding new supporters. Continually reach out, and find ways to make many different people happy working for your organization.

Plan for an increase

Not only should you insist on diversity in fundraising methods and staggered timing for efforts, but you should also write challenge into your fundraising plan. If you need to raise $100,000, and your five planned activities promise to generate that much, slip in an extra effort that might bring you 10% over goal. That offers the prospect of a truly growing fund and also takes the anxiety out of a year of hard work. If you stretch too high, volunteers may lose their spirit. But a little margin will ease potential cash flow problems and budget stress.

Value your loyal donors

Even with diverse methods, you may find yourselves focusing too much energy on "prospecting": bringing in new donors. Remember that your "old faithfuls" need special attention too. They are the people who have the potential to move up the giving pyramid. In seeing your organization perform well consistently, a regular donor should gradually give more.

Provide incentives for donors at all levels

To encourage donors to increase their gifts, you may decide to institute Giving Clubs. These groupings of donors set goals for each individual: after giving at $75 per year for several years, a donor may not have much motivation to give $100 unless invited to join the "Century Club" or some similar group. Donors like to see their friends listed along with them on segmented acknowledgement lists. Even the most modest donor usually likes to review the categories of donors on a program or plaque in your entry hall.

Be conservative in estimating receipts

Planning is not the phase for putting on the rose-colored glasses. Planning is the time for conservative, cautious ambition. Do not project a 30% increase in an event's receipts, or similar windfalls, unless you want to risk losing your volunteers. Everyone likes a challenge but no one likes to be set up for failure.

Besides the human element, you cannot risk overly ambitious projections. If receipts fall lower, you will be too far into the fund year to recoup and schedule a new effort.

Balance your risk

Everyone in your organization will soon be bored if you repeat the same proven methods year after year. Worse, your prospects and donors will get bored too, and bored prospects means less money. Do plan something new each year, or a new wrinkle in an old favorite, to keep fundraising fresh and timely.

On the other hand, a fund plan consisting of totally new efforts spells doom. Even if all the methods work, the anxiety of risk and the stress of developing new ideas in every effort will wear you out. If you've got a glut of hot ideas, spread your planning over a two- to three-year period and introduce new methods over time. Give yourselves time to learn, evaluate, digest and improve.

DEVELOPING THE PLAN

With all the above criteria in mind, actually developing the plan is easier than you might think. First, you need to gather as many ideas as possible. Next, narrow them down to the most promising and appropriate.

Many boards have a weakness for fundraising ideas. When it is not on the agenda, and immediate financial need is pressing, discussion will routinely degenerate into a wild flinging about of fundraising ideas. Staff may wring their hands and wonder where all these great ideas and enthusiasm were when they needed them, and what to do to halt useless discussion now that it is too late.

Board and volunteers really need to have an opportunity to explode with ideas like this, and the solution is to set aside a time for productive brainstorming early in the planning stage.

The Planning Meeting

Set a meeting with just a few agenda items: to generate many fundraising ideas, to weigh the suggestions, and to select no more than 6 to 8 projects with real potential for the year. With serious input in the early stages, board and volunteers will learn to channel their energies, and they will be far less likely to go off on tangents later in the year. Even better, they will think of ideas that have real money-raising potential in the community, faster than staff will.

At your planning meeting, post the goal for the year and the time frame, such as "$100,000 to be raised by December 31." Inform the participants of basics: the total budget, a very brief summary of antici-

With serious input in the early stages, board and volunteers will learn to channel their energies, and they will be far less likely to go off on tangents later in the year.

pated non-fund-raised income, and a quick review of previous fundraising efforts and the totals raised. Don't overburden them with figures, just give enough to justify the current need.

Start the meeting with a blackboard or flip charts. Have two note-takers: one to jot down all basic ideas on the chart or board, and one to take more extensive notes of the informal discussion around each idea, particularly the names of those most interested in each idea, who might potentially work on it.

You may already know the extent to which personal solicitation and mail appeals will take place. If so, jot them down on the big list. Then ask for ideas of other fundraisers: various types of events, phonothons, and so on. When suggestions are made for foundation grant proposals and major corporate appeals (other than local businesses), code them "S" for "staff effort." If you are a group composed entirely or primarily of volunteers, assign those tasks to a "Board Grants Committee." One way or another, keep business and foundation requests from becoming the focus of the brainstorming list. Those things must be done, when appropriate and promising, but they are long-term efforts and must not interfere with volunteer efforts to raise immediate, annual cash.

Write down every idea that comes up, practical or not. Write down all the variations on ideas. Let the brainstorming go on till there are far more ideas than you need, and only stop when it is clear that the quality and quantity of suggestions is declining.

A sample brainstorming list, unedited, might look like this:

mail campaign
personal solicitation
phonothon
benefit picnic
children's theatre show
holiday bazaar
refreshments at July 4 fireworks downtown
raffle a car
bottle collection drive
Halloween haunted house
grocery discount coupons
grant application to local fund
sell ads in newsletter or program
bake sales
board challenge fund
sell old equipment
spring fashion show
underwriters for events
discount coupon booklet sales
car wash

It would be a rare group that could do all these events, but nearly any group could develop this long a list in a brief brainstorming session! As you can easily see, some of these ideas require long planning, many volunteer hours, and high visibility. Some are quick, others are quiet or slow. All have variable fundraising capacity. With a list like this, you can begin to sort out priorities. Also, faced with a list, some reluctant volunteers will begin to face up to the reality of working on the annual fund, and most can find something they will enjoy.

Some of the ideas may immediately be discarded, but the rest need to be rated or selected. Depending on the responses you got, you might group similar ideas, or group projects that would occur at similar times of year. Try talking through the list and taking simple votes: perhaps you could place a plus (+) or minus (-) next to listings, with double pluses (++) for the best ideas. Those which are actually staff assignments (like the grant applications) should be marked "S" so they are not discarded for lack of interest.

Choosing the Best Ideas

Next, make a big chart to help in selecting the actual projects you will do. These are the issues you must weigh for each idea:

- Who will do the work?
- When would the project take place?
- How much planning time is involved?
- How much will it raise?
- Who is targeted for donations in each project?
- How much risk is involved?

These questions will help you test each idea against the criteria at the beginning of this chapter. The ultimate object is to find sufficient diverse projects to raise enough money to meet the goal, to involve many different workers without burdening any one individual or group, to spread the events over much of the fund year, to control overlap of planning time if the same workers are involved, and to achieve balance between the high- and low-risk projects. Chart these factors in the simplest form possible, so you can judge, as a group, the best and worst ideas. The brainstorm list above would be charted, as in Figure 1 on the following page.

You will usually find that, given the assignment of rating each of their ideas, the volunteers gathered will easily eliminate some of the less practical and profitable ideas. Even the time needed to chart those ideas will seem a waste. The best ideas will percolate to the top with little effort.

The rest of the ideas will need discussion. Concentrate decision-making factors on the key criteria. Can you make enough money on this project to justify the work, expense and volunteer time? Are there people willing to manage the project? Is there time enough to plan it? Is the project doable at the time it should occur? Is the risk worth the potential reward? A planning meeting run in this way is fun but exhausting. By the time you have narrowed things down to 6 to 12 ideas, you may be ready to take a break. Adjourn, and assign a small number of people to research the final ideas and to bring back projected timelines and recommendations for each of these ideas another day.

The next meeting should be only days or a week later. At that time, only discuss the finalist ideas. The time for brainstorming is over. Get to the specifics and details: who will chair each project, how many workers are needed, what dates are available, what expenses might be

Figure 2: Potential Fundraising Methods

Proposed Project	Time of Year	Amount of Planning	Who does the work	Potential $ goal	Risk rate	Community impact
mail campaign						
personal solicitation						
phonothon						
benefit picnic						
children's theatre						
holiday bazaar						
refreshments at July 4 Fireworks						
raffle a car						
bottle collection drive						
Halloween haunted house						
grocery discount coupons						
grant application to local fund						
sell ads in newsletter or program						
bake sales						
board challenge						
sell old equipment						
spring fashion show						
underwriters for events						
discount coupon booklet sales						
car wash						

Figure 3: Sample Chart for Analysis of Final Choices

Final Choices: Fund Plan
Fund Chairperson:

Planned Project	Date	Chair	Team Members	Expense	$Goal
mail campaign					
personal solicitation					
underwriters for events					
benefit concert					
benefit picnic					
raffle for car					
bake sales					

incurred in running each fundraiser and what can realistically be netted on each one. Based on this much more detailed and thoughtful analysis, your group should be ready to select the 4 to 8 methods and events that will make up your annual fund plan for the year. A new chart with more detail, such as the one above, will provide the type of analysis that will help in making your choices at this point.

SELECTING VOLUNTEER CHAIRS

Selection of an annual fund chairperson, a volunteer who will work closely with staff, and selection of volunteer chairs of each fundraising method or event are crucial at this point to assure progress. Not only do dinners, dances and carnivals need chairpeople, but mail campaigns, personal solicitation drives and phonothons need chairpeople too. Spread the assignments so there is a great deal of involvement without burden for any one person, and make certain that the overall annual fund chair is a person who can coordinate and communicate with them all. A balance of trust and ability to check up on people without offense is essential.

Reliable, organized people are your greatest asset; if you are short of these at this point, draw up a list of needs and brainstorm again. Among yourselves, think of people in the community who will be good at the specific events and assignments you have selected. Remember, if you don't have anyone ready and able to oversee a project, you can't do the project at all. Hopefully, you are just fleshing out basic committees at this point. Keep the assignments focused and defined.

When you start out looking for chairpeople, don't strong-arm anyone into a big task. If you have to make deals to get a chairperson, you are probably guaranteeing a lot more work for yourself down the line. A reluctant but otherwise "perfect" chairperson will be a burden for you. Keep looking till you find a willing chair. Compromise with a pair of co-chairpeople if you know they can work well together and complement each other, making up for each other's differences and weaknesses.

TIMELINES

After you've selected the methods and events for the entire year's plans, you are ready to create an overall timeline that will demonstrate precisely how the annual fund year will progress and how the projects will overlap and flow. (See Figure 4 on the facing page.) It is helpful to chart planned communications and membership activities as well, since those will have an impact on fundraising.

Plans are not meant to be guilt-inducing documents. They are . . . tools to help you select and focus on the highest potential activities possible.

For each fundraising project, you will need a timeline as well. For preliminary planning, a simple chart will help you visualize your commitment. As the planning progresses, this can be refined and detailed. (See Figure 5 on the facing page.)

By the time you complete this planning process, you will have a calendar of fundraising methods and events for the year, a projected total to be raised in keeping with need, and chairpeople and potential workers for each activity. If you have kept the original planning criteria in mind, you will also have assurance that you are meeting other needs as well, such as bringing in more prospects and attempting to raise maximum dollars from each donor.

There is a great deal of momentum from this activity. There's also a great sense of relief that all the ideas have been laid on the table, discussed and analyzed. People are usually ready to get moving toward real goals after this process and are willing to stop looking back to what "might have been." It is crucial that the momentum be continued through personal staff-board-volunteer contacts, thank-you notes to participants, timely assignments and progress reports.

Like all planning documents, your final chart will have to be revised and updated as the year progresses. In particular, you must continually check the actual amounts raised against the projections. Before you start the activities, determine the date at which you will have raised 50% of your goal, and then 75% and 90%. Check these particularly and, if you are not on target, reconvene the annual fund chairperson and the methods and events chairs, and adjust the plan.

Plans are not meant to be guilt-inducing documents. They are meant to be tools to help you select and focus on the highest potential activities possible. If one method falls short, feel lucky that you have done enough analysis to have sufficient information you need to boost other efforts and make up the difference. Consider your plan an integral part of a diverse annual fund operation which will, one way or another, succeed in meeting the goal.

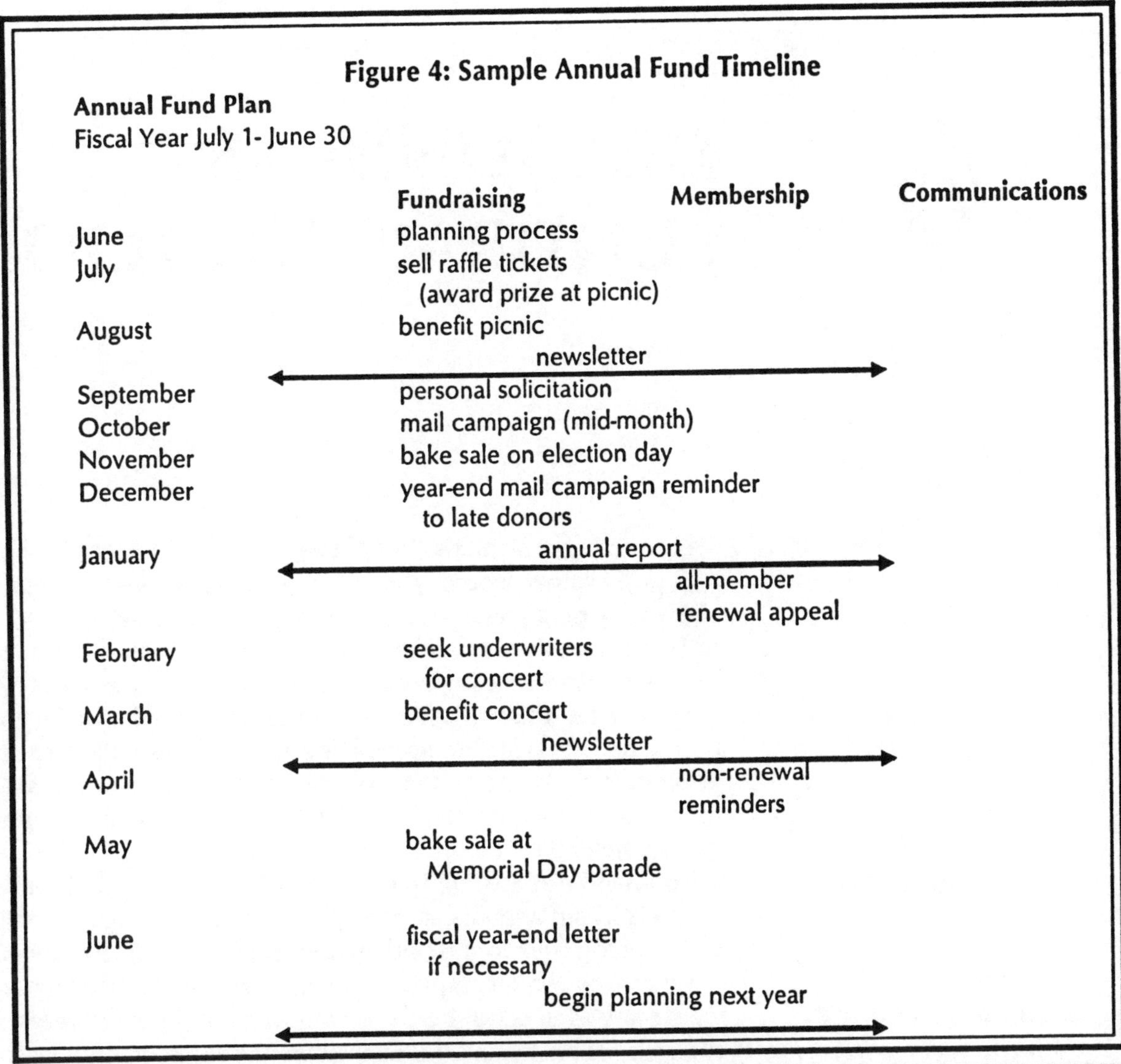

Figure 4: Sample Annual Fund Timeline

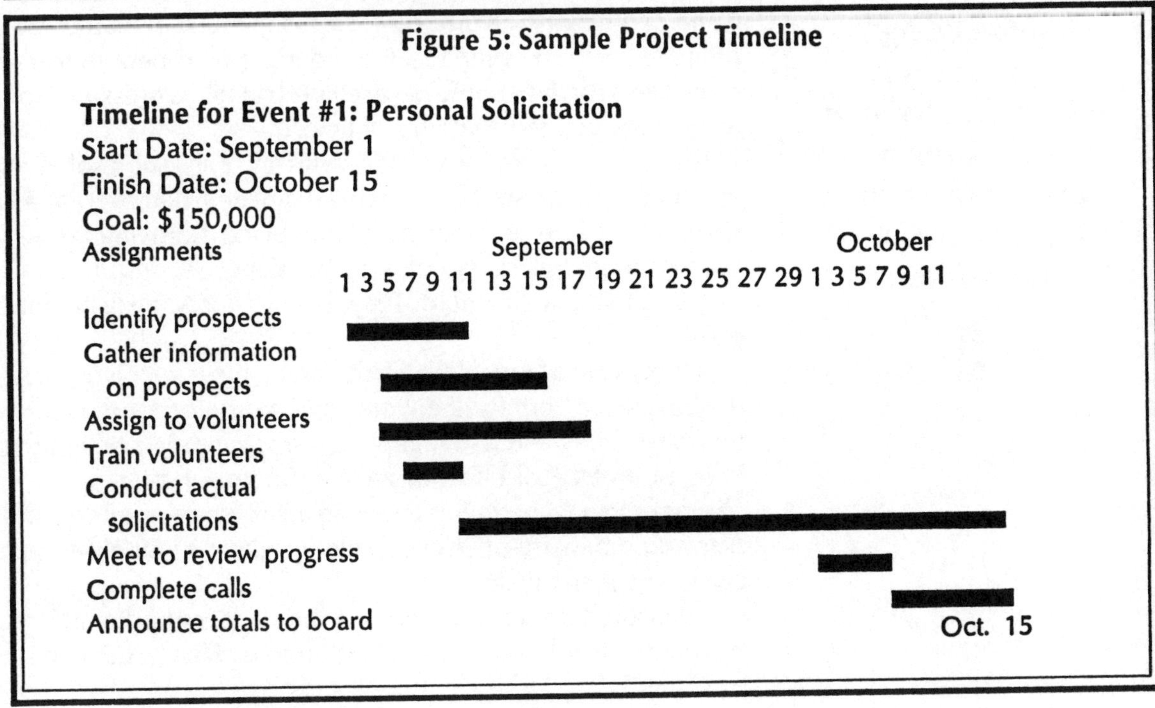

Figure 5: Sample Project Timeline

6 DEADLINES AS FUNDRAISING TOOLS

In strategic planning, people say "You will never get there if you don't know where you are going." Reaching the end of your fundraising project offers the same sort of quandary.

You must set a deadline for your annual fund drive, as you must for any fundraising campaign, because otherwise you will never finish. For one thing, you will never feel the campaign is finished if you do not have a definite deadline as well as a goal. But also, the last dollars will never come in till the end of the drive. You lose one of your great donor motivators if you don't have a deadline, because some people want to give at the end of the drive.

You need not assume that the deadline is the end of the year. Just because it's an annual campaign, you do not have to work all year on it. "Annual" refers to the budget it funds, not the time required.

When you run a campaign you are highly reliant on human beings, which means you will be the victim of every known preemptive and procrastination technique.

When you run a campaign you are highly reliant on human beings, which means you will be the victim of every known preemptive and procrastination technique. Even with the finest intentions, there are some people who cannot do their assignments until they are late, and others who must complete them early. Some people like to be first, some like to be last. Some people need deadline pressure. Some people need to know they've got lots of time.

The only way you can deal with all this, short of hiring a staff psychologist, is to set a reasonable deadline. Then everyone knows the rules of the game, and they all fall into place, satisfying their own needs. Most of them will be grateful for the deadline, despite the pressure it may add to the assignment. They need to know it will be done at some point.

In your role of organizer and official time-keeper, you must hope for the best, watch out for the worst, and worry for everyone. Procrastinators cannot be trusted to complete the assignments on time, so you will have to invest real effort in nagging them, or nagging the campaign chairman to nag them. But the deadline is your asset here, and because of it your otherwise-offensive reminders can be entirely acceptable. You can blame it on the deadline.

As for the budget, a deadline is the only assured method of getting the money in when you need it. You must have a deadline. You must publicize it along with the goal. You must use it as a tool to get the job done. If necessary, you can use it to deal with your own procrastination too!

There are hundreds of ways to use your deadline to help the campaign succeed. You'll think of more as you go along. Besides simply announcing and reiterating D-Day, consider these:

HAVE A DONATION COUNTDOWN TO DEADLINE

- Pick a deadline date that relates to your cause, for emphasis
- Tie the deadline date into an event, with announcement of success at the event
- Offer recognition to volunteers who complete their assignments first, last, within certain time periods, on dates related to the deadline
- Have donors set challenge gifts for completing before deadline
- Find a bank that will offer one-time interest hikes for campaign money invested before deadline
- Form teams of campaign workers who can compete against deadlines and each other

Remember that, beneath the fun and manipulation of these ideas, the deadline is an indispensable part of your campaign. It is the single most valuable key to your success, and in fact will be one of just two ways you can tell if you have reached success. By meeting your goal and meeting your deadline, you can feel pride, and give your volunteers a good rest before the next cycle begins.

7 WHERE WILL THE MONEY COME FROM?

I have yet to meet a nonprofit board that did not hope against hope that they could raise all their needed support from foundations and businesses. They see organizations as less scary prospects than people. And while diversity in sources is extremely important for long-term success, it is imperative that you and your entire organization understand that most contributions come from people. In your planning and your solicitations, put first things first, and start with your most reliable source.

PEOPLE

If you want to invest your time and effort most wisely, you will invest in individual donors. These are the people who care about your organization for their own personal reasons, and people who care about you. They are the only donors who can, consistently, write a check the date you ask for it, who can make decisions emotionally and even capriciously without submitting a request elsewhere, and who can do it year after year without justification to anyone else.

If your own commitment is strong (and it should be, for any effective nonprofit staffer), why would you want to spend all your time convincing institutions to support you? Isn't talking to people about shared personal convictions more interesting? Wouldn't you enjoy more personal gratification in obtaining a gift for purely charitable and philosophical reasons than for marketing reasons? Of course you will go for those business gifts too, but let me assure you that fundraising from businesses and foundations is no easier than it is from people, and it yields less over time.

Put first things first, and start with your most reliable source . . . people.

Research figures show repeatedly that at least 88% of the money donated for charitable causes in the United States each year comes from people. Individuals. The remaining 12% is split between businesses and foundations. If you have a finite amount of time and effort to invest in fundraising, attempt to allocate your time the same way: spend 88% of your time raising money from individuals, 6% with businesses and 6% with foundations.

You may say, "6% or 12% of my time will not be enough to get foundation grants or business gifts." But consider, will 6% or 12% of your goal be enough to keep you operating? Eighty-eight percent of your goal will get you mighty close to excellent, healthy operation. If it takes 50% of your time to raise 12% of your goal, you are wasting time.

People have a tendency to reinvest year after year, so with individual donors you are always building for the future. Businesses have a tendency to spread the wealth, and foundations have a tendency to fund the start-ups, so they are likely to move on to another nonprofit with their money in the future. If you are looking for an initial shot in the arm, try a business or a foundation. If you are looking for long-term, stable, communicative givers, try people.

Do not think that businesses and foundations should be removed from your prospect lists. They are excellent prospects for very particular parts of your operation. They may fund things you cannot hope to promote successfully with individuals. They offer valuable partnerships as well. They can be invaluable in augmenting your program, targeting new populations and developing new solutions to problems. But to succeed with your annual fund, you really must start with people. The bonus is that most businesses and foundations will be impressed by strong individual support of your campaign, and those "people" gifts may actually turn out to be a large part of the reason institutions give to you.

There are many methods for raising money from individuals, at every level of giving. Briefly, these include talking, writing and partying plus direct mail, phone solicitation and events. All these are appropriate for your annual appeal, and full utilization of diverse methods assures you of reaching the maximum potential donors. Your planning process should have identified which of these, and their multitudinous variations, will work best for your organization.

You will make a major step forward when you come to the point of saying, "OK, we understand and agree that individuals are our best prospects. Who are those individuals?" Now we are in business.

Identify the Prospects

Regardless of your overall goal, you will have prospects at every level of giving within the context of your goal. You will have Angels (also known as Heavy Hitters, Major Donors, Patrons, the Backbone of the Fund, and Best Friends). You will have mid-size donors (Old Faithfuls and People on the Way Up) and you'll have small donors (Grassroots Givers, the Masses, and the Key to your Future). You need each and every one of these individuals, and you need their giving levels represented equally well in each of your campaigns.

One of your jobs will be to maintain the loyalty of these givers while continually upgrading their gifts. At the same time, you must bring in new donors. Another job is to make each donor know how deeply you appreciate the support. These are all highly people-oriented assignments that take care and attention. A fundraiser's job, whether staff or volunteer, is always people-centered.

You know that only a percentage of those whom you ask for a gift will give it, but you can increase the likelihood of their giving through more personal attention and sensitivity to their interests and needs. You can also increase the effectiveness of your efforts by focusing on the best possible prospects from the beginning. First try to identify the broad groups that include your prospects, and then begin to segment them into potential giving capacity.

To identify broad groups of prospects, look for people who:

- are interested in your cause
- have sincere philanthropic intentions
- value community life

Narrow it down by selecting those who:

- participate in your organization's activities
- have given in the past
- have volunteered, now or in the past, to help
- volunteer or belong to similar organizations
- donate to similar organizations
- have benefitted from your service, or whose families have (if you are a social service organization, these may not be your best donors; if you are a cultural organization they will be)
- have served on your board, now or in the past
- have been, or are, on your staff

Your board should be involved in every aspect of your campaign, especially identification of prospects. Let them review all these compiled lists and add names and suggestions. A diverse board of directors will know people from every part of the community, and at a brainstorming meeting your list could grow geometrically.

Once you have a prospect list, treat it with care. This is your organization's private property, hard to come by and tailored to your needs. Don't trade it with another organization unless your board votes to do so after careful discussion. You know how resentful people are when magazines trade or sell lists to mail order houses. It isn't fair to your campaign or your prospects.

Build A Pyramid

Not all prospects are created equal, and it is essential that you determine, from the start, which ones have more capability to help you. As you have probably learned elsewhere, pyramids are very popular devices in fundraising, and you can learn to use them to your advantage both in finding groups of donors and in targeting capable individuals.

The typical pyramid, used especially in major campaigns, shows that the smallest number of donors give the largest dollar-size gifts, and that the largest number of donors give the smallest gifts. By building such a pyramid, you can figure out how many donors you need at each level of giving in order to reach your goal. The figure on this page shows how simple that is.

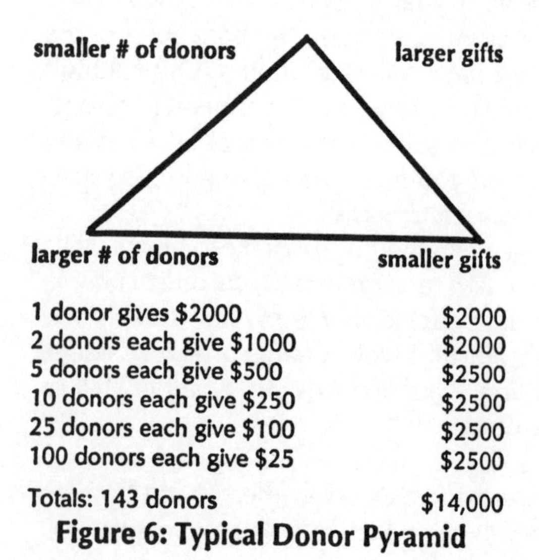

1 donor gives $2000	$2000
2 donors each give $1000	$2000
5 donors each give $500	$2500
10 donors each give $250	$2500
25 donors each give $100	$2500
100 donors each give $25	$2500
Totals: 143 donors	$14,000

Figure 6: Typical Donor Pyramid

Using the basic principal "fewer donors give larger gifts," you can play with this pyramid until it fits your

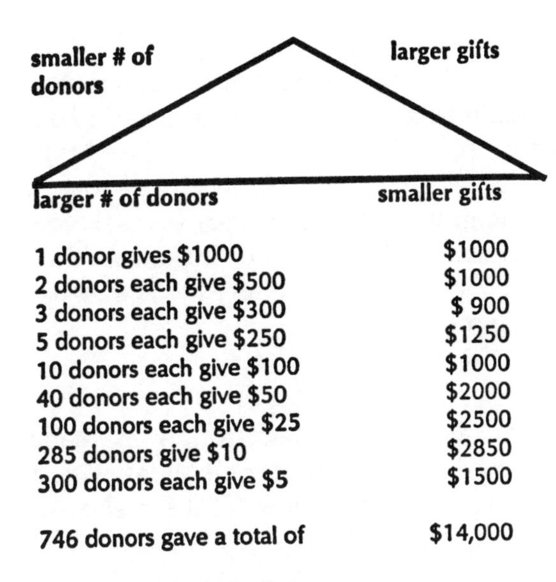

1 donor gives $1000	$1000
2 donors each give $500	$1000
3 donors each give $300	$ 900
5 donors each give $250	$1250
10 donors each give $100	$1000
40 donors each give $50	$2000
100 donors each give $25	$2500
285 donors give $10	$2850
300 donors each give $5	$1500
746 donors gave a total of	$14,000

Figure 7: Typical Grassroots Donor Pyramid

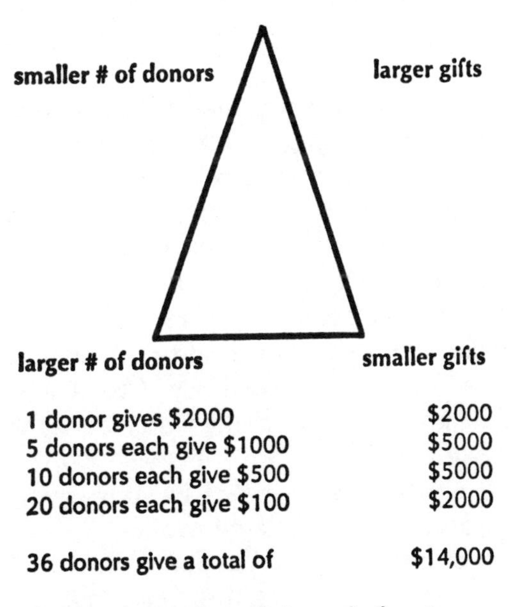

1 donor gives $2000	$2000
5 donors each give $1000	$5000
10 donors each give $500	$5000
20 donors each give $100	$2000
36 donors give a total of	$14,000

Figure 8: Alumni Association-type Pyramid

organization well. However, different types of organizations innately form different types of pyramids. Understanding the special character of your organization, and how that impacts on selection of prospects, will help you in targetting prospects.

While the triangle on the opposite page denotes a "typical" organization, your group is probably not perfectly typical. Consider a community-based, grassroots organization. You may receive far more than 50% of your funds from people at the lowest level of giving. Without them, your annual fund would be defunct. Your pyramid, realistically, will look more like the figure on this page at top left.

With a pyramid like this, you would concentrate efforts on fundraising methods that work best with large numbers, like direct mail, door-to-door and phone solicitation. You also can see that your primary effort is to bring new people in at the lower levels of giving in the largest numbers possible. And to make it work, you have to have a large market, albeit small donors.

Now consider another type of organization, such as a school alumni association. The possibility of bringing in new members at the lower levels is severely limited because the qualifications to enter the giving field are so tight: basically, only alumni of the school will choose to give to the fund. The big challenge, and the place for greatest effort, is in pushing people up the giving ladder, so that they are consistent donors year after year, giving larger and larger amounts. That pyramid might look like the figure on this page at bottom left.

Knowing what you do about your own group, you may be able to make a working guess at your pyramid; use it until the numbers begin to come in, and then adjust. In future years you can hone it down until it becomes entirely reflective of your current fundraising situation.

As you make deliberate and informed choices in fundraising, your pyramid will illustrate room for growth and improvement. You can select solicitors and fundraising methods based on the demographics of your audience, and adapt those choices when you decide to purposefully change or augment the group. You can also check yourselves; make sure you are not allowing the pyramid to rule your fundraising choices. The grassroots organization can often achieve a great growth spurt by focusing on moving low-level donors to higher giving levels, and the alumni-type organization can look for new ways to bring new donors in at the bottom of the pyramid.

Whatever the shape of your pyramid, you have two basic goals, each with emphasis appropriate to your organization. First, bring in new donors regularly. Enlarge your prospect pool with likely donors at every opportunity. (Even an alumni association could do this, by including parents and grandparents of alumni, summer students, continuing education students, and so on) Second, work your donors up the pyramid, encouraging increased gifts, at every opportunity. Proven donors are the most likely people to give larger gifts. Make the most of them: stay in touch, thank them, ask their opinions (and listen as well), include them in events, make sure they have your group well established in their list of organizations they not only give to, but appreciate year-round.

What About Tax Advantages?

You've certainly heard about the tax advantages of giving. Many donors have been able to combine charitable contributions with a remarkably good tax-saving plan, providing income for themselves or their families and giving sizeable gifts at far less cost to themselves than face value.

Note the "sizeable gifts" in that statement. Only major gifts carry a significant tax savings for the donor, regardless of the giving method. Your average $100 gift, regardless of tax deductibility, makes hardly a dent in the donor's tax bill.

If you are soliciting small gifts for the annual campaign, you may only need to remind donors that gifts are tax deductible to the full extent of the law, if they itemize. If you are soliciting larger gifts or gifts of property, or if such a gift appears on the scene unsolicited (as sometimes happens, believe it or not), you must help the donor get good advice.

Your assignment will be two-fold: to convince the donor that it will be gratifying to give away assets, and to convince the donor that you are the best recipient.

Sometimes donors can give tangible property, like real estate and art work, and seemingly fabricate tax savings out of thin air. If it looks that way to you, look again, with an accountant's or attorney's assistance. In particular, find a professional with experience in tax law. It changes often enough to keep us on our toes; for instance, in just the past year it has become possible for donors to deduct gifts of art and artifacts at current value regardless of their basis (original investment).

The truth of the matter is, no one ever gets richer giving away money. No matter what tax bracket your donor is in, he or she will be at least a little richer keeping money than giving it away. If that weren't true, all our organizations would be wealthy too!

The real, primary reason a donor gives is belief in your cause. Charitable intent must be the motivator to make a gift work.

Your assignment will be two-fold: to convince the donor that it will be gratifying to give away assets, and to convince the donor that you are the best recipient. If you concentrate on the latter, stress the good work you do and the better work you could do with more funds, the gratification will come along. If you start the conversation with emphasis on the overall benefits of giving not only are you taking a risk that the donor will pick some other recipient organization, but you are also treading on fairly unethical territory. You are not an investment counselor. You are a nonprofit advocate and will be far safer and more successful, too, if you stick with your primary purpose: your organization.

Tax law is designed to encourage charitable giving, but not to underwrite it. There are some planned giving promoters who currently market "good deal donations" with the focus on tax shelters. These promoters do not care which charity will get the donation. Resist making deals. Like any get-rich schemes, they are full of traps on all sides.

The real, primary reason a donor gives is belief in your cause. No one gets richer giving away money.

Once your donor has decided to give to you, you do have an obligation to help make that donation work to the maximum advantage for both of you. If you can show ways to take full advantage of existing tax incentives, your donor will be able to give you more dollars at less cost. Your gift may increase.

You can protect your potential gift by educating the prospect before he or she gets advice from his or her own advisors. Invite your organization's own accountant or attorney to discuss the gift with you and the donor. For one thing, your advisor is more likely to be a specialist in gifts and taxes.

When the donor's advisor gets involved, he or she will probably take the traditional tack and oppose the gift. Accountants and lawyers know well that nobody gets richer giving away money, and they are hired specifically to protect and increase principal. To do their jobs well, they must advise against overly generous giving. But remember, the money belongs to your donor. That's the person who should make the decision. Just help the donor get all sides of the story and all relevant information.

Finally, if you should become involved in a larger-sized gift, get professional help to represent your organization's interests as well. There are many things you may not know, and your naiveté will not help your generous donor. Make sure you learn who is responsible for appraisals (the donor is), whether you need appraisals (you probably won't for the gift records, but you will for insurance and other considerations), what gift forms to complete, and so on. You need good help on this, and it is money well spent. Think of it as part of showing appreciation for a gift, by treating it and the donor with care.

Your Prospects Are Your Friends

Some organizations treat their prospects like aliens. They act as if "those people" must be kept at a distance, treated with caution, given very little information so as to avoid bothering them and, even, feared. Volunteers who are afraid to do their solicitation assignments will cross the street rather than encounter their prospect.

Who could possibly feel good about an organization whose personnel or volunteers treat you as if you had a contagious disease? Remember, these prospects are your best hope for the future. More importantly, they became your prospects because you shared a commitment and concern for a cause, because you all have a sincere interest in bettering your community, and because it is likely that you are all working together to improve your lives.

Don't let fear of solicitation cause your volunteers to shun their prospects or to develop uncomfortable feelings about the organization. It is your responsibility to provide good training for solicitors so they can happily complete their assignments. You must be the ones to help the solicitors put their self-consciousness aside and ask on behalf of the organization. Show them that they are offering a prospect the opportunity to participate, to their best ability, in a worthwhile effort. Encourage your volunteers and your donors to become educated advocates of your organiztion.

You owe your prospects respect, kindness and appreciation. You should be frank and straightforward about the organization's needs when you solicit them, and grateful when they help. You should remember that it is the cause they are supporting, not your personal needs. Anytime you wonder how to deal with a prospect, put yourself in his or her place. How would you want to be treated? You and your prospects and donors are partners, working toward a shared goal.

One of the most remarkable aspects of the nonprofit world is the focus on others. Learn to spread that generosity of spirit, which you certainly have for the beneficiaries of your work, to your donors and prospects as well.

BUSINESSES

Enthusiasm for individual gifts should not totally discourage you from soliciting businesses. In businesses and business organizations, there is an increasing awareness of nonprofit needs and the value of community participation and societal changes, as well as the financial advantages of giving. Approached with the right perspective and the right methods, businesses can become a valuable part of your giving program.

It will help you to understand that businesses, unlike people, do not necessarily, or solely, give out of pure charitable intent. They will give first of all because it is good business. If it is not good for business, no strong charitable statements will make them change their minds. The business donor will approach a giving schedule as another aspect of the public relations/advertising program and will make gifts with marketing impact in mind. If this offends you, perhaps you should ask another member of the board or staff to handle business gifts. Remember that businesses have their mission, just as you do. While some are socially responsible, and have environmental or social goals, they ultimately must make money.

The business donor will approach a giving schedule as another aspect of the public relations/advertising program and will make gifts with marketing impact in mind.

Your best hope is to carefully select prospect businesses based not only on their capacity to give, but also on a match of their auxiliary goals with yours. Find ways to help them meet their goals through your organization's efforts or partnership.

You should design your approach to local and regional businesses after assessing their motivations. If you were a business owner, you might ask yourself these questions when considering a gift:

- How will our customers feel about this gift?
- How will our owners/partners/stockholders feel about this use of profits?
- Is this a cause that will attract or offend potential customers?
- Do we want to be publicly associated with this group of people?
- Can we use this gift to promote our business?

If you are the solicitor, you will increase your likelihood of getting the gift if you can demonstrate that:

- Customers would be sympathetic to the cause

- Potential customers would be more inclined to support a business that supported you
- Your board, volunteers and associates are the kind of people who would be a public asset
- Publicizing the gift will be an effective form of advertisement
- The cost, from net profit, will be considerably less than cash value of the gift, due to advertising benefit
- There is a natural affinity, a good match, between your organization and the business

There are certain types of gifts that businesses will be most inclined to make, and unfortunately not many of them are annual fund material. The nature of the annual fund is not very appealing to a business that wants to make some hay from its generosity. Helping pay for dull operating costs just doesn't make great news. They'd like to pay for:

- Pieces of equipment
- Special projects benefitting children and the elderly
- Community-impact projects
- Things and efforts that can be named
- High-visibility events
- Leverage

Consider this a challenge for your imagination, and try to find things in your regular operations budget that might adapt to those expenditures. For instance, maybe your social service organization could use a business gift to fund a gala fundraising event, unlike anything you could afford, and satisfy their desire to gain visibility, be associated with a social effort, and leverage funds at the same time. Similarly, businesses like to sponsor events; propose events you would have staged regardless of specific funding, but offer to give the business top billing in all advertisements and flyers as the "presentors." This is a tactic which started out with arts organizations but works very well in many fields.

You will do far better in seeking an annual gift by approaching the marketing department rather than the contributions department.

You will do far better in seeking an annual gift by approaching the marketing (advertising) department rather than the contributions department. Budgets for marketing will be immense compared to the contributions or "community relations" budget (if they even have one), and you will get a larger gift there, making a smaller dent in their budget. Besides, after answering the questions and making the case described above, you'll be able to show the rationale for including your group in the advertising budget.

Once you have determined which businesses are most likely to give, and therefore are worth an investment of your time, you proceed much as you would with individuals. If you know someone, or are asking for a major gift, you must try to get a face-to-face meeting and ask for the money in person. If you are looking for a smaller gift, farther down your giving pyramid, a letter or written proposal will do. But take advantage of any contacts you have, or can make, to learn who should get the request first, how much to ask for, and what the business might fund. Businesses often like to fund specific costs, which you should be able to find within your annual budget. Be prepared to offer examples of such funding opportunities.

A most important step with business contributions is the acknowledgment stage. It is very important that you demonstrate your appreciation, not just to management or owners but also to the public. Remember that a reason for making the gift was for public relations value. Let your donor get some mileage for the gift. You don't have to go overboard. This is business, after all, so you mustn't wax eloquent over a modest or disappointing gift. But your gratitude must equal their sacrifice.

There are many differences between individual contributions and business contributions, but the two major differences are the business's motivations and your signs of appreciation. If you uphold your end of the bargain, your business contributors will be loyal and your gifts will grow with their success. Over time, businesses will happily become key recruiters for other business gifts.

FOUNDATIONS

Yet another potential source of funds! This is the board's favorite target when money gets tight. Every board has heard a clamoring for foundation grants when need escalates, or when individual solicitation assignments are distributed.

Foundations, like businesses, are a wonderful source of funds under the right circumstances, and, like businesses, foundations will never take the place of individual gifts. Good fundraising for grants is hard work; it usually takes months to research and write proposals, and then more months to wait for the answer. Before you even get started, you have to determine whether or not the funds are appropriate for your annual fund.

With those warnings in hand, and an early start on individual fundraising already underway, you can plan your foundation grant search with the same basic approach you used for business: try to understand their motivations and needs.

Do not waste your time trying to mold a foundation to your purposes, or applying for a grant with disregard for its stated purpose.

Understand why the foundations exist, what they want to accomplish, and who runs them. Foundations have traditionally helped our society blaze new trails. Through the past century, foundations have joined others within the independent sector to stretch society in new directions. Probing studies, challenging research, new institutions and unsettling theories have all been funded by foundations and have rocked our societal assumptions. One of the reasons foundations are able to play this role is because they have relatively little at stake. Once the foundation is established, hurting egos have been boosted, tax burdens or budgets have been dealt with and customers and marketing have been cared for elsewhere. Foundations were generally started by people who had a strong charitable impulse, who had already provided well for their families, who had money to spare, and who had imaginations as well as the resources and energy to use them. Do not waste your time trying to mold an existing foundation to your purposes, or applying for a grant with disregard for its stated purpose. Foundations are secure and headstrong. But, when your purposes match, they can help you reach new heights.

Within a basic premise of independence and determination, each foundation is unique. Even with a great project, a photocopied proposal sent to a score of foundations will not do you any good. To succeed at foundation grantsmanship, you are obligated to start at the beginning, researching your prospects. Similar to your prospect identification with individuals, this is your method for pinpointing those foundations most aligned with your purposes and inclined to support your dreams.

To select prospective foundations you will need to talk with other nonprofits, plow through the development research department of a major library, contact the Foundation Center, read 990 tax forms in your state library, make phone calls, ask your board for information and generally play detective. If you don't have the time to do this right, don't cut corners; instead, hire a consultant to do the research for you. Unless you have unlimited funds for outside contractors, or absolutely cannot write, or the grant application requires scores of pages and technical descriptions, you are wiser to hire a consultant to help at the research stage than at the writing stage. This is the key to saving time and energy and still getting the maximum grant support later. You must find the handful of foundations best suited to you before you start preparing proposals.

Further time can be saved by prioritizing your handful of prospects with these questions:

- What is the mission of the foundation?
- What aspects of our operations suit the foundation guidelines best?
- Are we philosophically and politically alike, or will our opposites attract?
- Is there anything in our annual operations expense that is within their granting interests?
- Are we planning a special project or acquisition that would suit them, or would we have to bend our plans?

Foundations lean toward projects, not operations. They tend to fund start-ups, innovations, short-term projects, experiments and some risk ventures. Most foundations limit the number of years or projects they will support for any one organization, with the exception of those groups that may be named in their guidelines for annual grants. You must never belittle your operations budget or change your plans simply to accept a grant. That is irresponsible. You would be relinquishing control of your organization's future in trade for short-term financial comfort.

There is a place for foundation support in nearly every nonprofit. When you do become seriously involved in grant seeking, you should get good educational help for your staff who will be involved. Refer to the list of readings at the end of this book, but also remember:

- Do your research first
- Make personal contact with the foundation
- Follow the directions!
- Write clear, direct proposals
- Don't make promises you cannot keep
- Stay within your mission
- Give yourself plenty of time before deadlines

- Let others in your organization know what you are asking for
- Thank, and report back to, the foundation
- Never, ever, budget for grant income before you know if your proposal was funded.

Section Three ■ Proven Fundraising Methods

This may be the section you have been waiting for. "Don't burden me with all this other stuff," you say. "Just tell me how to do it!" The following suggestions are proven methods of fundraising, and there is not a miracle drug among them. But with the right planning, leadership, and perseverance, these are the methods that will work best for your annual fund.

8 THE ART OF PERSONAL SOLICITATION

There is no source of funds as promising as individuals. When you and your board and volunteers have faced up to this reality, you will be ready to use your time and attention most effectively in personal solicitation. You will have many methods to choose from, even within the relatively narrow structure of personal contact. But the first step is to eliminate, or lessen, the fears and trepidations we all have about asking for money.

Always remember:

- The mission is key.
- You are not asking for yourself.
- Treat your prospect with respect and kindness.
- Individuals make their own choices: you offer opportunities.

Understand that you can only offer the opportunity. Sometimes it will work better than your greatest hopes. Sometimes you will be disappointed and will have to try again.

There are ways to make asking for money easier, and many suggestions follow. However, the best way is to practice, and that should be part of your fundraising from the beginning. Practice on each other first, starting with practice role-playing sessions, and proceding to in-house solicitations of board and staff. Then stay in practice by asking a number of people each fund year. Don't consider solicitation a task that anyone is excused from.

BEFORE YOU SOLICIT

You must learn to distinguish between adequate preparation for

Identify ✔

Cultivate ✔

Solicit ✔

solicitation and avoidance through overpreparation. Take time to know your prospects, and learn the value of cultivation. Then, when you are prepared—but still a little anxious—know the value of ASKING.

The two biggest problems in individual solicitation are 1) identifying the prospects and 2) asking for the gift. When you get to the large-gift or major-gift stage, these problems are magnified. You cannot expect to get big gifts from people who do not have personal resources, and you cannot expect able donors to respond, with major gifts, to direct mail approaches.

When you need big gifts, you need to adapt your efforts. Keep in mind the importance of identification and cultivation before solicitation. These are interrelated tasks, and each builds on the other. You are never finished!

Identification

Through personal suggestions, research techniques, and review of organizational records, you will be able to identify those prospects and donors who can give at increasingly higher amounts. Sometimes you will have to make some assumptions, but as you gain experience you'll find that prospects give you clues and reveal their own capability and commitment to giving.

You build your major prospect file, in almost all cases, by learning more about your current donors. When, occasionally, you find a new prospect who may be interested in your efforts but has not given before, you have to start from scratch, learning all you can about that person's interests and inclinations.

Rate your prospects twice . . . once for capability, then for inclination.

Focus on two criteria in identifying your best prospects. This is considered "rating" prospects, and is done by all serious development operations. Even a small organization can do rating, based on advice of volunteers and board members, combined with staff knowledge and any research you can gather. It need not be the distasteful task some consider it. You can start by developing a simple scale for rating people's capability to give, with someone able to give the highest gift in your campaign rated "1" and someone able to give at the lowest level rated "8." Save the number "9" for people who are unrated, due to insufficient information. Remember that the rating is for *capability* and has nothing to do with *inclination* to give at that level.

Add to this financial capability figure a second rating that measures commitment to your cause. Rate your most devoted donors and volunteers "A"; rate those who support you consistently but have at least one bigger interest "B"; rate those who occasionally give but really don't have a keen awareness of your efforts "C"; and rate those who are disinclined to give to your organization and perhaps to others like you, "D." With this simple method, your rating sheet might look like Figure 9 on the facing page.

You can use this list to organize your solicitation, depending upon your goals. If you need to gather a strong volunteer group first, you might enlist Capt. Hook and Betsy Ross, since they don't have the highest financial capability but are so interested in the cause that they will help out.

Figure 9: Prospect Rating System (CONFIDENTIAL)

Capacity
1 = $5000 or more
2 = $2500–4999
3 = $1000–2499
4 = $500–999
5 = $250–499
6 = $100–249
7 = $ 50–99
8 = under $50
9 = undetermined

Commitment
A = totally involved
B = devoted, but has another primary interest
C = occasional donor
D = uninterested

Prospect	Financial Capability	Commitment
Ms. Betsy Ross	3	A
Mr and Mrs. J. Adams	1	D
Mr. and Ms. Hancock	2	A
Dr. Doolittle	2	B
Capt. Hook	5	A
Mr. G. Washington	1	B

In looking for a major gift, it is easy to decide where to start. The choice between Adams and Washington is clear: both can afford a major gift, but Washington has a higher level of interest. Washington becomes your first assignment. Depending on other needs, you might decide to solicit the Hancocks before the Adamses as well. Though their capability is lower, the Hancocks have such a high level of interest that you will probably do best with them.

Even an experienced fundraiser is less comfortable during a solicitation assignment if the amount to ask for is unclear. It really helps to have a dollar goal.

After rating your prospects, inform the solicitors of important background information. A simple print-out will provide information that is most useful. (See Figure 10 on the following page.) Volunteers should be aware of this information before soliciting, but should also be aware of the confidentiality of this data. Be certain it will not be misused.

Even an experienced fundraiser is less comfortable during a solicitation assignment if the amount to ask for is unclear. It really helps to have a dollar goal. All the research you can do will contribute to your ability to determine the correct amount to ask for, and that will be key to your success. Identifying donors is not just learning their names, it is identifying their potential niche in the organization.

Cultivation

Cultivation is preparing your prospect to be asked and raising his or her willingness to support your organization. While more concentrated effort may be made for your high-level prospects, for instance, your "As" and "Bs," this is necessary at all levels.

Public relations, social gatherings, and in-house mailings are just the beginning of your effort to communicate with prospects. You then must deepen your involvement with donors, members, and prospects with

Figure 10: Sample Donor/Prospect Information

(*attach address label if you have one*) Rating:______

name address city, state zip	Gift History prior to 1993 :
	1989: annual ___________
source of prospect ___________	membership ______
type of prospect ___________	other ___________
business or employment ___________	1990: annual ___________
connection to organization:	membership ______
	other ___________
	1991: annual ___________
	membership ______
	other ___________
	1992: annual ___________
special notes:	membership ______
	other ___________

A solicitation call consists of just a few key steps: Plan, Focus, Listen, Ask, and Thank. Then Follow-up, and later, Repeat.

more personal approaches. Asking someone to become involved as a volunteer is a way to draw him or her into the cause, as is an invitation to an educational or social event or a private conversation. For each prospect, you must tailor your communications to provide them information and growing commitment in the way they will be most comfortable.

In your year-round plan, in addition to scheduling actual fundraising events and solicitations, you should develop a cultivation schedule. This becomes particularly important when you foresee a major campaign in the next several years, but it is also important in raising annual fund donor gifts to higher levels. Your calendar for cultivation might look like Figure 11 on the facing page.

In this plan, people are asked to become members and also to give to the annual appeal, but they are given many other opportunities to forge connections with the organization. By the time September's solicitation arrives, the new prospects are fairly familiar with the organization and are primed for the opportunity to help. Equally important, current donors have been kept informed, and volunteers have been given both assignments and recognition.

Solicitation

This is, of course, the final step to getting the gift. It's also the way to get ideas for new prospects, more volunteer involvement, creative thinking about organizational goals, and perhaps enlist a new solicitor. We each go on a call with the goal of raising money, but may return with many special gifts, from time to enthusiasm.

Naturally, the success we hope for in solicitation is getting the gift, but it is also important that you and your prospect both leave the

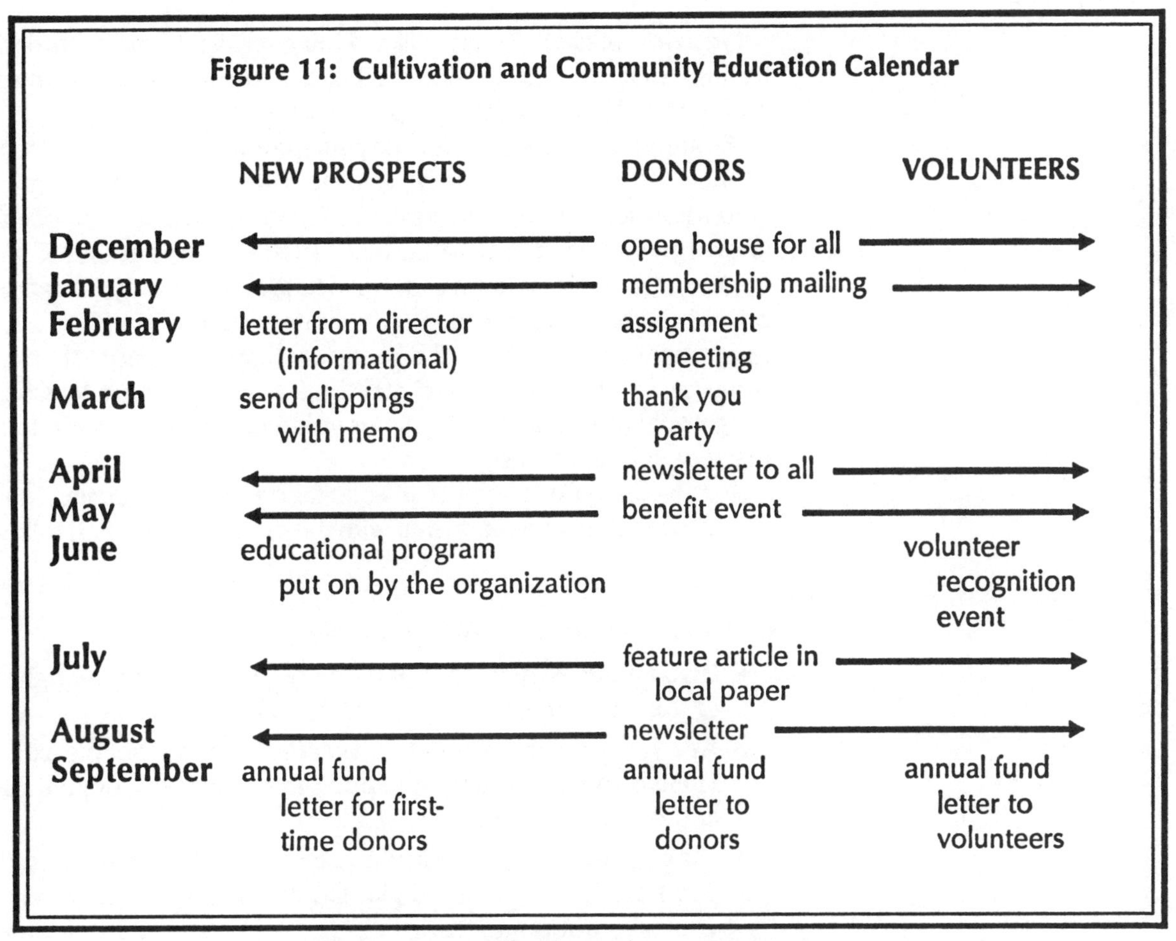

Figure 11: Cultivation and Community Education Calendar

	NEW PROSPECTS	DONORS	VOLUNTEERS
December	←	open house for all	→
January	←	membership mailing	→
February	letter from director (informational)	assignment meeting	
March	send clippings with memo	thank you party	
April	←	newsletter to all	→
May	←	benefit event	→
June	educational program put on by the organization		volunteer recognition event
July	←	feature article in local paper	→
August	←	newsletter	→
September	annual fund letter for first-time donors	annual fund letter to donors	annual fund letter to volunteers

appointment with a few other successes:

- mutual commitment to the organization
- respect for each other
- a sense of cooperative progress toward a goal

Each solicitation is one part gift-getting and one part future-building. Try to think of your assignment in that way, and your job will be easier and more enjoyable.

It will be easier for you to complete your assignment if you do these preparations:

- Know your organization and project
- Know your donor
- Have a positive mental attitude
- Feel energetic, fed and rested
- Have a goal

When you talk with your prospect:

- Listen to his/her thoughts and opinions
- Understand the other point of view
- Find the motivations of your prospect
- Show some heart and spirit in your request
- Don't take objections or complaints personally; don't be defensive
- Give the request adequate time, but don't waste time

No two solicitations are alike. However, you can be prepared by having adequate information, laying the groundwork, staying flexible during the call, and finishing up with sincere thanks.

Some of the greatest effort of your staff fundraiser, or the chairman of the fundraising committee, will be in training and preparing your volunteers to conduct successful solicitations. Do not expect them to know how to do this or to be comfortable with it at first. Give every opportunity for learning. Also, do not give too many assignments at once. It is reasonable to think a volunteer could complete five to ten assignments a year; you will be safest assigning no more than three. In some cases, with new board members or people new to solicitation, assign only one. Check up on your volunteer, coach, congratulate and reassign in a timely fashion.

It may help you to approach solicitation chronologically. Make sure your prospect has a relationship with the organization, then follow these steps:

Chronology of a Solicitation Call

- **Plan ahead:** Stay in control of the situation: solicit the right person at the right time, when you are prepared.
- **Ask for an appointment in advance**: Don't do the solicitation WHILE you are setting the appointment, but do let your prospect know it will happen later. Be fair.
- **Make your own gift first:** You cannot be a convincing solicitor if you have not yet made a gift. Don't ask anyone to do something you have not done. It will help you feel good about asking.
- **Arrive on time.**
- **Bring a few selected pieces of information:** a case statement, a statement of need, a budget, whatever is appropriate to your request. The material should be thorough without being overwhelming.
- **Focus on the issues:** Get to the subject and stick to it.
- **Be friendly, not gossipy.**
- **Praise your effort:** Don't belittle the assignment. Say positive things about your organization and your assignment. Treat it like an *opportunity* for you and for the prospect. Don't invite the prospect to say no.
- **Be respectful**, and treat your prospect like an intelligent, caring human being.
- **Listen:** Care about your prospect's thoughts and concerns. Answer questions if you can, and promise to get the answers if you can't. Listening, and really hearing the other's thoughts, is the most important part of any conversation, especially this one!
- **Ask for the gift!** If you think you may have trouble doing this, bring a partner along who can discipline you or step in to ask if you falter.
- **Discuss the ways of making the gift:** cash, pledges, partial payments, etc. If planned gifts such as real estate and bequests are suggested, offer to help find professional assistance: don't accept

this gift on the spot unless you went in to ask for it!

- **Close the conversation before it gets boring.**
- **Be grateful:** Say thank you. Tell how you will follow-up and confirm the gift.
- **Afterwards!** Be thoughtful of those who will follow you next year. When you leave, write down a brief summary of the meeting and give it to your campaign chairman or staff member. Report back to the office and make certain all follow-up is assigned.
- **Always write a personal note of thanks** for the appointment and your prospect's attention and, of course, for their gift or pledge.

Always be generous in your acknowledgment of efforts and your expressions of thanks for work, regardless of the results!

In general, it will help to make your conversation personal. Tell about your own choices: why you give your time to the organization, and why you made a contribution. There is no reason why a solicitation should take longer than 45 minutes; shorter is fine too.

To sum it up, a solicitation call consists of just a few key steps: Plan, Focus, Listen, Ask, and Thank. Then Follow-up, and later, Repeat.

Each contact with a prospect will yield you information that can be used in strategizing the best possible solicitation. Be very careful that valuable information, seemingly unimportant in a brief conversation, is not lost.

A little anxiety before an assignment is not all bad. Like any important performance or activity, the stress of solicitation will cause nervousness. But that is also a way to insure that you try your hardest, value the opportunity, and concentrate. Alleviate all the unnecessary fears, but don't lose the edge of excitement that helps you do well! Based on nervous trainee solicitors, the chart below may serve as a helpful guide.

Do's and Don'ts for a Solicitation Call

Do:

- be well-prepared
- make sure you are the right one for the assignment
- bring information with you
- know about the campaign
- be committed to the project
- make your own gift first
- be candid about your reasons for calling/meeting
- understand the possibilities for pledging
- get the gift OR make a specific date to get it
- thank the prospect for both the gift and his or her time

Don't:

- squeeze your request in at an inopportune time
- solicit for two organizations at once
- talk for too long
- say "We have you down for..."
- leave without some answer or commitment
- make a lunch or cocktail appointment for solicitation

- get discouraged

Remember that people:

- need to know the goals
- like to feel part of a positive movement
- will only pay attention for a short time
- are flattered to be asked

Also: Your confidence in the project will make the difference.

- Make your gift first; make sure it is meaningful in terms of the project and your ability to give. Giving comes from the heart: rationalization comes later.
- No one ever got richer by giving money away, nor do they expect to! Listen, and encourage dialogue. Answer questions. State the case first, ask for the gift second. Aim high!
- DON'T GET DISCOURAGED. LOTS OF GIFTS TAKE MORE THAN ONE REQUEST.

Ask your staff and your volunteers to complete a "Call Report" each time they conclude an appointment with a prospect. A sample Call Report should encourage information on both the prospect and any other new prospects who might pop up in conversation. A sample is illustrated in Figure 12 on the facing page.

State the case . . . ask for the gift, aim high!

While you are thanking your donor for the resulting gift, you will be returning to the beginning of this continuum, with identification efforts on new prospects and added information on the current prospect. Listen when you solicit. The information you are given may be as valuable as the gift!

The most frequent complaint from members and staff of nonprofit boards and organizations is "most of our board members say they'll do anything EXCEPT fundraising. And that's what we need most!" This is a serious problem which is perpetuated by boards that simply refuse to deal with it, or who postpone making changes.

Very few grow to love fundraising solicitation, but many people become very good at it. They thrive on the tremendous satisfaction of having helped an important cause. Don't promise your solicitors fun: promise them pride of accomplishment in knowing your goals are closer to being met. Anyone can be a good fundraiser. The spirit is the most important criteria, and the training can easily be provided.

First, resolve immediately to include fundraising in a careful job description for prospective board members. No one should be asked to serve on a board without a full understanding of the responsibilities involved.

Next, you can try some of the following:

- schedule a budget discussion followed by a fundraising planning session, so the need is perfectly clear
- explore, in a board meeting, the many forms of fundraising available to your organization, and the many roles that must be filled by volunteers
- be open to options suggested by others
- ask a board member who has had success in some areas of

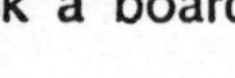

Figure 12: Donor/Prospect Call Report

name
address
city, state zip

source of prospect________________
type of prospect________________
business or employment________________
connection to the organization:

Gift History
prior to 1994:

1993: annual__________
membership__________
other__________
1992: __________
1991: __________

After talking with your prospects please complete this form and return to the organization.

Date and time of contact:

Type of contact (phone, in person, letter):

Request amount? Actual donation:

How did the prospect feel about the organization ?

Any suggestions to improve the organization?

Could we be asking for more? or did we aim too high?

Other remarks on your conversation?

Were any other people suggested as donors or volunteers?

What follow-up from the office is appropriate?

Signed: Date:

fundraising FOR YOUR ORGANIZATION to talk on behalf of taking assignments

- ask someone else to come to talk to your board about fundraising: either a professional, or someone from another board who has had good luck. It's always great to get someone who was a reluctant beginner
- give the board chairman a lot of information and support in learning about fundraising
- make fundraising a regular agenda item at each meeting
- talk to board members individually and learn what kind of objections they have. Try to work with them, outside of board meetings, to develop manageable, gratifying assignments
- give very small assignments at first, and call soon after to see how the board member is progressing
- give a lot of positive reinforcement and hand-holding
- offer to go along on a call or help in other tangible ways
- always be certain that your board members have all the information they need to complete assignments

Always be generous in your acknowledgment of efforts and your expressions of thanks for work, regardless of the results!

Look upon volunteer solicitation as a long-term goal of your organization. Make your own internal planning calendar of ways to bring the board closer to 100% participation in fundraising. This is not a change that you can make in a few weeks or even months, but the difference over a period of years will be demonstrated dramatically in your ability to meet an increasing budget.

9 FUNDRAISING BY PERSONAL MAIL

While you always stand a better chance of getting a large donation when you ask in person, that is not a practical approach in the majority of cases. You have to find another way to reach large numbers of people. As everyone with a mailing address in this country knows, solicitation by mail is the most popular way.

There are two basic approaches for mail solicitation. One is personalized mail, and the other is direct mail. In all fundraising, the more personalized approach is always more effective. Therefore, you should aim for as much personalization as possible. However, direct mail also serves excellent purposes and may help you. Direct mail will be discussed in the next chapter.

Personalized requests generally go to people you have identified as potential donors because of their individual activities, interests, contacts and friends. Recall your giving pyramids, and target the middle-level donors for personalized mail solicitation. You may personalize the letter itself, in the text, or at least include an inside address, real signature, and a real stamp on the envelope. The goal is to contact individuals who have been pre-identified as prospects, and to ask them to give. Depending upon the mailing itself, the request, and the donor history of your prospects, you might expect a response level of 8%-10% for new donors or as much as 70% for renewing donors.

Direct mail generally is sent to individuals who are identified because they are part of a larger group, and that group has been identified as likely donors. In direct mail, lists are purchased for fundraising, and huge numbers of letters are sent at reduced bulk postage rates. A response level of 1%-2% is considered excellent for direct mail. To make this work, you must have access to large, appropriate lists, the capability to put out large mailings, and a need for continuing influx of new donors at low levels. Direct mail is a donor recruitment device that pays off in the long term by bringing donors in at the low, wide end of the pyramid.

If direct mail is not the right choice for your group, find another way to approach the people at the bottom of the pyramid. Rather than send nonpersonalized letters to everyone, you might choose to have an event that brings you new prospects and involves people in your cause;

you might have a raffle and use the names and addresses of all ticket buyers for a prospect mailing later; you might gather names and donations at the door to your facility or event. The purpose of this activity is to gather more prospects who would actually be interested in a more personalized approach later.

You will have to make choices in your fundraising plan. For a community group, the personalized mail approach must be your first avenue, after face-to-face solicitation. For a regional or national group, direct mail may be the first choice, but it should not supplant serious personalized mail programs.

You cannot do everything. Pick the activities that make best use of your strengths (good volunteers, free printing, etc.) and are most likely to yield enough money to meet goal.

CREATING A PERSONALIZED MAILING PROGRAM

Step 1 DEVELOP YOUR PROSPECT LIST

Much of your initial work on mail solicitation is already done if you have invested real effort in reviewing and building a prospect list for personal solicitation. You probably found hundreds of people who might give to your organization, but were not such good prospects to justify the time and effort of a face-to-face solicitation. All those people are appropriate for a mail campaign. In addition, you can develop a larger list with volunteer help.

Much of your initial work on mail solicitation is already done if you have invested real effort in reviewing and building a prospect list for personal solicitation.

It is well worth your time to gather board members and volunteers at small meetings simply to develop your lists. Not only look for new names, but call on their personal knowledge of the community to revise addresses, delete the names of those who have moved or died, and to add new residents. Take to such a meeting:

- Programs, donor lists and other acknowledgements of donors who may have given to similar causes, in your region
- Chamber of Commerce Membership lists
- Phone books, including yellow pages
- Expired donor or membership lists from your organization

At your list-generation meetings, encourage volunteers to talk among themselves as they review copies of your current lists, and assign one person to write down names. The object is to get a basic list that you can start with. Brainstorming will be the most effective method, and it is also fun for all the participants. Be prepared later to go through the list and find addresses, which can be very time consuming. Unless you have a very tiny goal, you will need to sort the prospects according to potential gifts. Build your ideal giving pyramid, creating various giving levels. Then, divide your prospect list into about four categories such as "under $50," "$50-$100," "$101-$250" and "$251-$500." Volunteers can easily and quickly help you rate prospects, with a good list and codes. Most helpers are most comfortable if this is fairly confidential; later in major campaigns you may find that your volunteers will discuss ratings more openly.

For each organization and each campaign, these ranges will be different, but remember that your highest level prospects do not belong on this list! They must be asked face-to-face. Later, you will be able to revise the pyramid based on the actual prospects who donate. In this way you will learn more about segmenting your list effectively.

The reason for dividing your list into categories is to allow you greater fundraising capability later. It is best to ask for a specific amount in your request, and by creating "Giving Clubs" or levels of giving, you offer each donor a personal challenge to increase his or her support regularly. In order to utilize Giving Clubs best, you must segment your prospect list.

But even if you do not choose to promote Giving Clubs now, letters that target a gift range will be most successful. Donors need to know what you would like them to do.

Step 2 GATHER GOOD MATERIALS

You will need printed materials: at the least, letterheads, envelopes, and gift envelopes or pledge cards. If your budget allows it, add a brochure, flyer, or case statement. Do not compromise effective materials, but also do not become a conspicuous spender at the print shop. Potential donors need to see materials that are tasteful and effective. At the same time, they need to see evidence of your cost-effectiveness. Remember a few things in gathering materials:

- Donors need clear information they can absorb quickly.
- You are looking for unrestricted money, so do not focus on just one program or need.
- Your overall concept of yourselves will be revealed in your materials, so test it on several non-staff and non-board people first.

The return gift envelope is tremendously important. People use these envelopes, and even save them for months (sometimes years!) till they are ready to give. Even if your request letter is quickly tossed out, the gift envelope stands as a reminder.

Most average givers write contribution checks at the end of each month, once they see how much cash they have left over. While this is not the kind of thinking that produces the most generous annual gifts, it does mean that a return envelope in the pile of bills will serve as reminder. Knowing this about your donors may help you decide what day of the month to send your mailing. It may also encourage your search for new ways to teach people about giving a truly "annual" gift, which should consider your operational needs for a year, not a month.

The most common return envelopes, called Business Reply Envelopes, or BREs, have a long flap which allows more print and information on the inside. Since you will have to pay for two-sided printing simply to make the envelope work for you, make the most of the opportunity. The inside panels can be used for information-gathering, with the top inside panel asking for suggestions, names, or other information. See a sample envelope in Figure 13 on the next page.

Naturally, you will want to make all this material as tailored to your organization as possible, but this is a start. Do make sure that you suggest the right gift amounts. If an average gift in your community is $35, do not list $25 and $50 as the only choices. Even the strongest-willed people often think they must do just what a printed document says.

Figure 13: Sample Gift Return Envelope

(Brief sentence on special accomplishments last year)

Please suggest any friends who might be interested in learning more about our activities:

____

____

____

- -

(fold)

Yes, we'd like to help support the Annual Fund
with a gift of **$25____ $50____ $100______ $250______ $500________other__________**

Name: ____
Address: ____
City, State, Zip: ____________________________________

Thank you so much for your contribution, which is tax deductible to the extent of the law.

On the outside flaps, consider printing your logo or an attractive photo appropriate to your projects, on the back. It is a great way to use a picture to reemphasize your request. On the front, print your organization's mailing address. Some groups affix stamps to these envelopes or print them prepaid so the donor will not have to use a stamp. Most donors seem to feel that paying for a stamp is a small expense and dislike the thought of considerable loss to the organization. If you don't know what to do, send an unstamped, BRE envelope. No one will criticize it, and it costs the least.

Step 3 WRITE A GOOD LETTER

Your letter is crucial. Work the draft over many times. No matter what you are asking for, you must include these items:

- an explanation of the organization
- description of the need
- a concrete request for a gift
- tax deductibility information
- thanks

Make sure your letter comes from the heart, and effectively conveys the spirit of the cause as well as the sincerity of the need. Make sure you actually ask for the gift!! Remember details too, such as a date on the letter, a REAL signature if at all possible, and a P.S. (Marketing experts have learned that the P.S. is the most frequently read portion of the letter.)

Short letter or long letter: that is the constant question. Nonprofits seem to follow magazine subscription marketing trends, and right now the trend is for multipage letters. But if you ask your donors, you will find that they prefer one-page letters. They also prefer that you not waste paper and other resources. You can say it all in one page, and the donor is most likely to read it in shorter format.

Practice writing your own letter, but test it against the basic idea illustrated in Figure 14 below.

Figure 14: Sample Donor Letter

Name
Address
City, State, Zip

(Include inside address if you can afford it.)

Dear (Name): *(If you can't personalize, at least make the salutation individual: Dear Friend, Dear Helper, Dear Art Lover, etc.)*

Why you are writing — *you share an interest.*

What is the cause, and the case for support — *even a regular donor should be reminded.*

How your group will be responsible in using the gift — *state successes, cost-effectiveness, low administrative expenses.*

Where they can see evidence of the gift's usefulness — *explain who the ultimate recipients are; let the donor share your pride in advancing the cause.*

The amount you hope he or she will give — *where to send it, that it is tax deductible.*

Express your gratitude.

Signature — (*personal if possible*)

P.S. *Studies have proven that the postscript is the most frequently read portion of any letter. If you lose your reader above, you've still got a chance down here. Use it!*

In a short letter, every word is important, but the request is especially so! The biggest mistake, and the most frequent, is that solicitors forget to ASK.

The next best way to get the whole letter read is to start with a personal statement. Tell how you feel. Tell how the work is making other people feel. Convey a sense of energy and spirit. A fundraising letter has a lot of work to do, and it needs help from humans!

Step 4 INVOLVE YOUR BOARD AND VOLUNTEERS IN THE MAILING

First of all, this means asking volunteers to fold, stuff, stamp, sign and mail the letters. They can have a good time doing this and be very useful. But if you don't have surplus volunteers, or this is not a good use of time for those available, consider using local volunteer groups, particularly senior citizens. In many communities, the senior groups may offer mailing preparation as a regular contribution. If so, they may be able to hand-address your letters, which is wonderful. Hand-written mail is read more frequently than typed. Labels, and the horrid new window envelopes for fundraising, scream "impersonal!"

The biggest reason people don't give is that they are not asked!

Regardless of hands-on involvement, update your board on the progress of the mail campaign. If certain volunteers signed letters and added personal comments (a sure way to increase returns), be sure you let them know about the success of their own efforts.

Let the motivation for the campaign come from the board. Trust the board to share your concern. People only live up to their responsibilities when you expect them to do so.

Step 5 ESTABLISH AND MAINTAIN GOOD RECORDS

Write down every piece of information uncovered by your mailing. These things are the ground work for your next, more ambitious, appeal.

Make sure you update computer listings with every piece of mail that comes back, either post-office returns or gift return envelopes.

Be sure you add all newly suggested names to your lists.

Record all gifts and thank donors daily.

Step 6 FOLLOW UP EVERY APPEAL AND THANK, THANK, THANK!

In keeping with the idea of matching thank-you styles to soliciting sytles, write a letter of thanks in response to these gifts. Every donor, and every potential donor who does not give this time, should continue to get careful attention from you. Most importantly, thank every donor immediately upon receipt of the gift or the pledge. You cannot thank a donor too often, or too kindly.

Some donors will ask to remain anonymous, and you must respect those wishes. But no amount of anonymity makes recognition impossible. There are hundreds of ways to recognize a donor, with public attention or very private thanks. Be sure you have recognized your donors appropriately and graciously, perhaps even frequently, before you ask them for a subsequent gift.

Step 7 WRITE DOWN WHAT YOU LEARN

As you go through the campaign, you will think of hundreds of lessons that will make your next campaign easier and more successful.

Write everything down and keep it in a reasonable order. Next year you, or your successor, will be delighted that you did not trust your memory. Figure 15 below shows a sample schedule for personalized mail solicitation.

Fig. 15: Sample Personalized Mail Solicitation Schedule

ANNUAL FUND: SAMPLE SCHEDULE FOR PERSONALIZED MAIL SOLICITATION

Week One:
order new printing of flyer
order letterhead and envelopes for mailing
order extra return-mail gift envelopes
order borrowed, purchased and/or traded mailing lists

Week Two:
address envelopes (by hand or machine)
write the fundraising letter and have it printed

Week Three:
complete envelope addressing (grouped by capability
if you are segmenting your mailing)

Week Four : Board Meeting
distribute personal solicitation assignments and deadlines
select, sign letters and stuff envelopes to by-mail
prospects

Week Five:
mail all letters
(at the same time, follow up on any loose ends for personal solicitation.....
it should be completed by the time the mailing goes out)

Week Seven:
send out the first progress report on personal solicitations
completed and gifts coming in through the mail
begin sending weekly reports

Week Twelve:
send reminders to best prospects

Week Twenty:
final report : Celebrate!

10 FUNDRAISING BY DIRECT MAIL

If you go into a direct mail program with the right expectations, it will work very well for you. If you use direct mail to solicit high-level, or even middle-level, donors in a community organization, you will be disappointed.

The primary purpose of direct mail is not to bring in the highest dollar gifts; it is to identify and attract new donors. You may spend quite a lot of money, per donor, for the responses you get in direct mail. But if you can hold on to those donors for several years, and increase their giving through other kinds of fundraising efforts, the original investment will be worth it.

In some ways, direct mail works just like personalized mail. Many confuse the two and think they are doing "direct" mail when they send any request letter. The steps to direct mail are:

Step 1 DEVELOP YOUR MAILING LIST

In this case, you need not know your prospects. More important is their similarity to your "typical" donor. You may rent or purchase mailing lists of magazine subscribers, catalog buyers, voters, donors to other groups, and hundreds of other categories. Before you start shopping for a list, determine the characteristics of your best donor prospect, such as: age, residence, personal interests, education level, political persuasion, family size, and so on. If you have access to a study of members of organizations like yours, use it to help target your prospects.

Be aware that most mailing lists are rented for a single use. Most are purchased in quantity, sorted by zip codes. You can negotiate with the mailing house for the precise selection you need. Don't buy batches of zip codes you don't need. The price is per thousand listings, and it can really add up. While you may not have the time or sophistication to do this, be aware that many groups buy the lists only for zip codes in more wealthy areas. If you know those areas, select them.

Step 2 GATHER MATERIALS FOR THE MAILING

Most of the people who receive your direct mail appeal will know very little about your organization, if anything. They will spend very little time looking over the materials. So, while a little simplicity might work very well in a smaller group of personalized requests, you may have to be more blatant and showy with direct mail. You may choose to use color, slick paper or inserts of stickers, photos, or "gifts" like bookmarks printed with your logo. You only have a few seconds to grab the direct mail reader's attention.

Direct mail offers you an opportunity to learn a lot. You can send different packages of print material to similar mailing lists, or even alternate two packages within single zip codes (package 1 to last name initials A-L, package 2 to the M-Z). If you are prepared to evaluate and refine your efforts, don't miss the chance to test with each mailing.

The primary purpose of direct mail is not to bring in the highest dollar gifts; it is to identify and attract new donors.

Don't let a fancy marketing firm convince you to create a package of materials that does not "feel" right to you. Few marketing firms work with nonprofits often enough to learn the fine differences between nonprofit and profit operations. Understand that you need to hear all their advice and need to know about their experience with other nonprofits, but then make choices that seem comfortable and ethical to you.

Many groups now offer charge-card payments for contributions, and some offer a monthly payment plan for charge-card users. Either way, you will probably receive more contributions if you offer charge card use, and you may get larger gifts. However, you have to decide whether you have sufficient volume to justify the trouble, and whether you have sufficient staff to handle the new task. Also try to determine if your donors will consider it a convenience, or a sign that you have lost the "human touch." If the latter, it may not be worth it.

Step 3 WRITE A GOOD LETTER

You can write your own letter for direct mail, if you can write it for other appeals. You know your prospects best, and probably can come closest to appealing to them. However, direct mail is really a speciality, and if you can get some marketing help (pro bono, if possible!) listen to the suggestions well. Try to find a balance between admiring marketing professionalism and believing in your own knowledge and good sense.

Make sure the letter really speaks to the type of reader who receives it. If you selected the mailing list for a particular reason, emphasize it: for instance, "We know that parents of infants are concerned about..." or "As a resident of the valley, you are probably concerned with ....." Counteract the coolness of a direct mail package and try to include a purely human message; using an example of one individual benefiting from your program will be most effective.

Consider testing your mail appeal by using two or more different letters, if the numbers are large enough to show trends. To find any statistical indications, you need to test at least hundreds, preferably thousands, of prospects. While you can get wonderful gift responses from 20, 30 or 40 people, you cannot make assumptions about large group behaviors based on such small numbers, with just one result such as a donation (as opposed to a complex questionnaire or personalized focus group).

A test can be very useful in developing the next appeal. Be sure you create a coding system that will allow you to evaluate the responses to each letter.

Be especially clear with your request. Let the reader know what you want and how to do it. Use the postscript to reemphasize the level of gift you are seeking and the tax deductibility. Be certain you include a return gift envelope.

Step 4 OVERSEE THE MAILING

Make sure you've included yourself, at your home address, in the list as a test. If your letter does not arrive when you expect it, double check everything.

When you do direct mail, you will probably deal with larger numbers of envelopes than you want to process in your own office. A mailing house will receive the labels direct from your mailing list supplier, can receive your printed materials direct from the printer, and you can be almost oblivious of the pressures of getting the mail out on time.

But don't relax! Plenty of things go wrong between the delivery of labels and print materials and the stuffing, posting and mailing. Take a trip to the mail house and see for yourself that they are stuffing the correct materials, or have them send you a sample. Double check the mailing date. Make sure you've included yourself, at your home address, in the list as a test. If your letter does not arrive when you expect it, double check everything.

When mail starts coming back, note the date. If it is later than you would have anticipated, talk with the mail house to make sure the mailing was on time. If responses are slow, or nonexistent, call the mail house and check up on progress. If your job is small compared to others, it could disappear for weeks!

Step 5 EVALUATE RESPONSE

Be certain to keep accurate records of response dates and rates from your direct mail appeal. This is essential to improving your effort next year. Remember that it is not just the dollars you are looking for. You need to know the numbers who responded and which mailing lists worked best if you used more than one at a time.

You can analyze the demographics of your respondents, and determine whether certain zip codes worked best for you. If your mailing had different letters, with slightly different messages, compare them as well. Learn all you can, then do your next mailing with lists more pinpointed than the first.

Step 6 FOLLOW UP AND THANK, THANK, THANK!

One place where there is no difference in fundraising methods is in thanking. The respondent to a direct mail piece should receive thanks promptly and appreciatively. If you can personalize it a bit, do so. This is already the beginning of moving that donor up the giving pyramid.

Step 7 WRITE DOWN WHAT YOU LEARN

Direct mail is a science, and it is constantly being refined. There is no way you will be able to remember what you learn in getting out a direct mail appeal unless you write it down. And always remember, people move around a lot in the development field, not just staff, but board members too. So think of the next person in line. Leave a little education in the files.

Throughout all fundraising mailing, there is a need to keep good records, be organized and timely, and to keep track of many assignments at once. You may find a few methods that work well for you, and those are the ones you should use. There's no perfect way to stay on target for a mail campaign, other than constant effort and organization.

11 FUNDRAISING BY PHONE

There are at least five ways to raise money using your telephone. The first, never to be forgotten, is a personal call by an individual solicitor, asking for a gift. While face-to-face meetings are most effective, the phone, when used by a friend, is a next best step.

Your choices for fundraising with the telephone include personal calls, phonothons, telemarketing, telethons (and radiothons) and, the newest, 900 numbers. Personal calls really fall within the realm of personal solicitation, though it is important always to recognize that face-to-face solicitation is always preferable.

Outside of a personal call, the simplest, and least expensive, is the phonothon. In a phonothon, you gather your volunteers together at one site with many telephones and make calls to many of your donors or potential donors asking for their contributions. These can be new donors, renewing members, lapsed donors or members, or donors at a particular dollar level. You can select the target group, but make sure it is a good match with your phone volunteers.

When the telephone was first used for fundraising purposes, it was highly effective, in no small part because of its surprise value.

In telemarketing, you hire an outside firm to do the same thing. You provide them with prospects' names and phone numbers, and their paid staff people telephone your prospects and ask them to give to your annual fund.

In telethons and radiothons, a television or radio show focuses on your fundraising effort and encourages people to phone and make contributions as pledges.

Now the "900" number has been created and is opening up a new fundraising method. The "900" number is a call with a fixed price, similar to the no-cost "800" numbers. For fundraising, this number can be promoted and donors can make the call, use a charge-card for donation, and the cost of the phone call is automatically billed.

When the telephone was first used for fundraising purposes, it was highly effective, in no small part because of its surprise value. People were pleased to hear from their friends who called on behalf of an organization. Old classmates, former board members, community friends who see each other seldom, were all pleased to hear from each other and exchange a little bit of news and ask for a gift at the same time. However, fundraising by telephone has become big business and now almost all of us are annoyed to pick up the phone in the evening and hear another solicitation.

There are ways that you can still use the telephone in a highly effective manner, but you must plan carefully and you must be highly sensitive to your donor's wishes. Also, there are certain kinds of fundraising that will be more effective by phone than others.

You will probably get your highest response rate in telephone solicitation by pairing callers and donors with close relationships. An old college classmate, calling someone she hasn't seen in 15 years, has a very good chance of receiving a pledge or a gift over the phone. People who know each other well and who feel a sense of kindness toward each other will treat each other well on the phone and will take a request for funds seriously.

If you are "cold calling," which means calling people you do not know and who do not have a relationship with your organization, you will only receive a very small percentage of pledges. However, you may be able to make up for this by volume. If you can call two thousand people in a night, even if you only get 50 new donors, you'll be doing very well. Those 50 people may be people you could never have reached in any other way. However, if you were using volunteer callers, they might be very discouraged by these numbers and lose willingness to volunteer again later.

This is where telemarketing comes in. Businesses have made a very good business out of cold calling. Paid phoners do not mind the turn-downs that they receive. They simply treat it as a job and go on to the next phone call. So if you want to develop a membership through cold calling, perhaps you should use paid, well-trained phoners. If you want to get a high percentage yield on your calls, and your prospects include people closely related to your organization, use volunteers.

If you're in a big city or an area served by a cable network, or if you have access to a community television station that is well watched, you might want to try a telethon. Jerry Lewis is the dean of all telethons, and you can take a lesson in running a telethon by watching his annual program in September. However, don't be misled into thinking that all the money shown on the boards during the televised telethons is really being raised at that moment. A large percentage of the money reported during a televised telethon is money that has been raised year-round through many different kinds of efforts, including corporate fundraising. Only the very few final dollars are actually raised on television. You should keep this in mind if you are trying to plan a telethon yourselves. No matter what kind of "thon" you plan, be sure to have some success to report to keep your callers' spirits high.

No matter what kind of "thon" you plan, be sure to have some success to report to keep your callers' spirits high.

Most groups that have little or no experience with telephone fundraising should approach the idea with enthusiasm but caution. Most importantly, think of the phone methods as just one part of your overall fundraising plan.

Be realistic. Don't expect a killing in one night. Remember that each new donor is a step in the right direction. It's one more person with a human contact to your organization, one more person getting practice in writing checks to your fund, and one more person who has a feeling for helping you and your cause. Each call makes a new friend, and a good many of them will bring you new dollars. A great investment in your future.

CONSIDERATE PHONOTHONS

Every organization could benefit by including more consideration for prospects in its phonothon planning. If you are a community organization, there's all the more reason to be thoughtful: your callers will see their prospects daily following the fundraiser. Good starter rules for phonothons include those listed below.

Tips for Successful Phonothons

- Consider your solicitors' and prospects' sensitivities.
- Give prospects the opportunity to avoid a phone call by making a pledge in advance. Encourage a gentle but straightforward approach on the telephone. Have friends call their friends.
- Do not call during the dinner hour.
- Avoid conflicts with scheduled community activities, voting, special TV shows, and traditional activities.
- Provide a written script for your phoners.
- Provide good information for your phoners so they can answer questions.
- Keep the energy level high at the phonothon base, with food and constant updates on pledge progress.
- Make sure each of your phoners makes his or her own gift before picking up the phone.
- Don't ask for major gifts over the phone.
- Offer your phoners clerical assistance, by teaming up pairs of callers.
- Have more people than there are telephones.
- Keep everybody close together so they can hear others talking.
- Show your workers just as much appreciation as you show your donors.
- Try to raise only a percentage of your annual fund through the phonothon, and target the percentage in advance.

From these suggestions, you can see that the keys to success are good planning, consideration, many hands (and voices) working, and reasonable expectations.

Before the Phonothon

- **Get a good location.** A bank, brokerage firm, phone company, law office, or another site with many phone lines will work best. Try to arrange free use of phones with charges only for long-distance calls. Find a comfortable, central location with easy parking. Remember, just having a lot of telephones is not enough; your site must have enough different phones lines going out so that many callers can work concurrently. Make sure you can serve food and beverages.

- **Choose the best evenings.** Tuesday, Wednesday and Thursday, 6:30-9:00 p.m., have traditionally proven most productive. Many groups are successful in calling on Sunday afternoons. Beware of local and national holidays, all religious holidays, high-interest sports activities, and very popular television specials. Particularly avoid family times such as the dinner hour, Sunday morning and evening, and high-stress times like early mornings.
- **Allow four to six weeks to recruit volunteers.** Recruit one-third more helpers than you need, because some will not show up, and plan to have double the number of workers as phones. This way people can take turns with a partner, making the calls and writing the thank-you notes, or the shy people can take the clerical jobs.
- **Remind volunteers one week in advance,** and on the day before the phonothon.
- **Plan for food and drink.** This is a real key to a good evening. The better the food, the more congenial your volunteers will be. Decide whether you feel comfortable asking volunteers to bring food. If not, have a staff member take responsibility, but in no case overlook treats!
- **Ask a photographer to come.** It makes it an event and can be useful later on for PR.
- **Compile a good prospect list**. Decide whom you will focus on: new prospects, faithful donors, lapsed members, $10 donors, and so on. This may provide you with a theme and your callers with a "good excuse" if the prospects ask why they are being called. It also gives you a logical and manageable way to prepare the lists.
- **Provide your callers with neat, thorough information.** They need concrete information on the organization, the budget, the annual fund, the membership rules, and the amount given by each donor last year. Occasionally, they will need the donor's full giving history (if you are asking for larger gifts, or increases). They also need each prospect's name, address, phone number, and relationship to the organization.
- **Develop a pledge card** that can record the necessary information and be sent the next day to the people who pledged. Make sure you keep carbons or photocopies for your files. Don't print any confidential information about the caller or the conversation on the copy that goes to your donor.
- **Put together packets of printed materials,** including blank letter-head or other thank-you notes and summary sheets so the calling teams can document each phone call and thank each pledging donor as they work through their lists.
- **Send a postcard to all prospective donors** several weeks prior to the phonothon and offer them the opportunity to give immediately to avoid being called. State the time and date of the planned phonothon, and promise that you'll remove their name from the evening's calling if they send a contribution immediately. This

works wonderfully!

- **Arrange in advance for a "clean-up crew"** that will stay late and tidy up the site. Workers do not want to arrive at work in the morning to find dirty cups, miscellaneous papers and doodles, and food crumbs on their desks!
- **Check in with your site a day or two in advance** and make certain they have remembered. Make sure you know how to get into the building if it is usually locked, where your volunteers should park, where you should set up food or plug in coffee pots, and most importantly, how to use the phones! Find out if you should keep written logs of all calls made, or all long-distance calls. Be appreciative and cooperative.
- **Purchase stamps in advance** so you can mail all the pledges and thank-you cards when you leave the phonothon. Your prospects will be thanked, and receive their pledge reminder, while the call is still fresh in their minds.

During the Phonothon

Each caller should have a packet with pens, note pad, matching gift or other informative pamphlets, facts about the organization, answers to anticipated questions and thank-you notes. Be prepared with extras.

Train Your Volunteers! Don't make any assumptions about the knowledge, comfort level, or conversational ability of your callers. Your brief introduction should include:

Don't make any assumptions about the knowledge, comfort level, or conversational ability of your callers.

- The mission of the organization
- The total funds needed, and the goal for the phonothon
- Explanation of packet of materials and prospect information
- Confidentiality
- How to use the phones
- Recommended script and length of calls
- How to create written records and thank-you notes
- Teamwork
- A demonstration or brief role play
- Encouragement

Ask your volunteers for pledges! Anyone who has not yet given to the fund should make a pledge or gift before starting to make calls. Commitment shows in the voice!

Assign rovers to gather information and continually update a big visible progress report. The same people can refresh supplies of information, thank-you notes and stamps. This is a good job for staff or experienced volunteers, because the rovers will also answer many extra questions and do a lot of hand-holding.

Set goals. Set one overall phonothon goal, and a goal for each phoning session. Also, set goals for calls in each gift category, such as new donors, lapsed donors, and so on. Callers should feel free to talk about the organization. Build their enthusiasm and knowledge in the training session and you'll garner as much in good public relations as in donations.

An energetic phonothon should last two and one-half to three hours, unless you've provided for new troops of callers to arrive and take over mid-way. It's too much to ask anyone to talk non-stop for more than three hours.

Ask your volunteers to fill out questionnaires before they leave, with suggestions to improve your next phonothon. And if you have another scheduled for the very next night, try to implement changes immediately.

After the Phonothon

On your way home, mail all completed thank-you notes to contributors.

Write down everything you learned. All your mistakes, your great ideas, your successes, the things the volunteers liked, the good and bad aspects of the site, how the volunteers liked the refreshments, the general energy and spirit of the event, and anything else that seems relevant.

Compute your statistics. You and your volunteers will be more gratified if you know:

- number and dollar amount of specified pledges
- number of unspecified pledges
- total number of prospects reached
- number of people not home
- number of people who could not or would not give
- average amount of pledge.

Send a summary of results, along with a personal thank-you note, to each volunteer who worked on any phase of your phonothon. Remember to thank them for any pledges they personally made the night of the phonothon too.

Before you do the phonothon next year, review your notes and revamp your planning to include suggestions and lessons learned. A sample phonothon checklist is shown in Figure 16 on the next page.

Keep a Positive Attitude

Remember that statistics have shown that 5% of your prospects are truly unable to give, and as many as 50% won't be home. Experience also shows that pledges of unspecified amounts may add up to as much as 50% of the total raised!

Keep your options open for other forms of fundraising in addition to the phonothon. Different people respond to different approaches. The more methods you use, the more donors you will attract.

Fig. 16: Phonothon Checklist

PHONOTHON PLANNING CHECKLIST ☑

- ☐ **Reserve the location**
  name of facility:
  address:
  contact person:
  number of phones:
  entrance door:
  parking area:
- ☐ **Set the date**
  time:
  day of week:
- ☐ **Recruit volunteers** (need at least 2x number of phones)
  confirm in writing:
  reminder day before phonothon:
- ☐ **Send Early Warning to Prospects**: suggest advance gifts
- ☐ **Refreshments**
  supplied by:
  food:
  beverage:
  paper supplies:
- ☐ **Recruit clean-up crew**
- ☐ **Compile Prospect List**
  organize information for callers
- ☐ **Gather information for callers**
- ☐ **Gather pledge and thank-you materials** (including stamps)
- ☐ **Bring easel or other materials for running totals**
- ☐ **Photographer or other documentation**
- ☐ **Check with site two days in advance**
- ☐ **Solicit the volunteers:** get pledges from each one
- ☐ **Train your volunteers well**
- ☐ **Thank your volunteers and your in-kind donors!**

12 FUNDRAISING WITH EVENTS

To some people, fundraising is synonomous with special events. It is true that some small community organizations start out simply through funds raised in special events. But events, and the related raffles, games, auctions and others, are very tricky as dependable sources of a majority of your income on a regular basis. Do plan special events, and make the most of them, but diversify your annual fund.

When you are able to stage a special event with volunteer labor, you are most likely to make a profit. That is how most events start out. For a larger organization, however, it may begin to seem necessary to have staff do much of the work, or wise to hire professional assistance to run an event; then the profit quickly dwindles. The dollar value of volunteer help is enormous and is always undervalued until you begin to pay someone a reasonable fee for the same activities.

If you are looking for ways to draw many prospects into the bottom of your giving pyramid, an event can be an excellent method.

The best special events have many bonus side effects. Events offer wonderful publicity, both prior to and during the occasion. The work involved tends to bring staff, volunteers, board and community together in a rewarding way which leaves a feeling of generosity and goodwill. It is possible to use an event, carefully, to help change or mold community opinion regarding your organization. And events are an excellent way to make use of enthusiastic supporters who might not be able to make a significant financial contribution. If you are looking for ways to draw many prospects into the bottom of your giving pyramid, an event can be an excellent method.

Events need to be planned carefully, if not cautiously. In the momentary excitment about a new idea, be sure not to be swept into the complexities of running the event before you have determined that it is the right kind of project, will meet real, predetermined goals, and that you have sufficient volunteer help to pull it off.

Early in the discussion of an event, determine its appropriateness for your organization. It may be difficult for you to understand how the community will view your event, since you may be excited and see the prospect of great profit. But the image projected by a single event can enhance or destroy all the public relations efforts of the past few years. Do not attempt to make money on any activity that suggests your mission is weak. For instance, a Las Vegas Night might be considered in poor taste to support a local counseling center that is dealing with problems of addiction in the community. A circus with trained animals might be inappropriate for a Humane Society event. Try to look at your project with perspective, and understand the message you will give the community.

During your annual fund planning process, special events probably were suggested, and selected, as a source of some percentage of your annual goal. As you begin to brainstorm event ideas, keep that goal in mind. Do you need to raise it all on one event, or would several smaller projects be more feasible? Who will be responsible for the project? Will it distract from the annual fund efforts that promise far greater dollar rewards?

Enthusiasm for an event is essential to carry you all through the planning and work of a special event. But enthusiasm is not enough. Someone on the planning team has to look over the hot new idea with a cool eye to timing, resources and goal, before you can jump in without reserve. Without trying to dampen spirits, ask these questions:

Enthusiasm for an event is essential to carry you all through the planning and work of a special event. But enthusiasm is not enough.

- How much do we need to raise in special events this year?
- What is a reasonable goal for this suggested event?
- What fixed expenses will be incurred?
- Do we have enough volunteers to run the event?
- How much staff time will it take?
- Will the event interfere with timing or staff for other annual fund activities?
- Is there enough interest, and money, in the community to make this event successful?
- Are there competing events, at the same time, or similar types of events, that might interfere?
- What image of our organization will this event promote?

If you are considering a large event, it would be wise to have a small planning committee review these questions and bring them back to the board or fundraising committee before a final decision is made. Simple matters like choice of date can make or break an event, and a planning committee can consider all options and make strong recommendations.

The planning committee, after determining that the event is appropriate and worthwhile, should begin to sketch out the plan:

- What is the event?
- When will it occur?
- What benefits will it bring the organization?
- What is the dollar goal for the event?
- Who will serve on the committee?
- Who will chair the event?
- What tasks will require staff involvement?

A key part of the planning committee's efforts should be the development of a budget. Many volunteer event committees do not do this, and just slide through without any idea of fixed costs or potential losses.

Even a totally volunteer event will end up costing something, and that should be determined at the outset. Fixed costs will be incurred regardless of attendance, such as advertising and facility rental, and can devastate hope for a profit if too much risk is involved. Budget carefully, and provide for contingencies as much as possible.

Once you have settled these preliminary considerations, the most important attributes of a good event are:

- Strong leadership
- Sufficient volunteer crew
- Excellent organization
- Timing
- Enthusiasm
- Good publicity
- Community support and attendance

The majority of special events, though very successful the first few times, lose appeal after the third year.

Try to select a chairperson who has experience in running events and who is good at getting other people organized and working. A good chair makes all the difference.

If you run the same event several years in a row, beware the three-year mark, both for leadership and the event itself. The majority of special events, though very successful the first few times, lose appeal after the third year. If you find a decline in profits and volunteer enthusiasm after year three, find a new event. In the same sense, if your chairperson is "gung ho" in year one, runs a professional quality event in year two, and seems burned out year three, accept his or her retirement gracefully. Don't doggedly stick it out in either circumstance, because the life of a fading event can seldom be extended.

If you do an event once and the response is poor, volunteers seem worn out, and even the original promoters seem bored, give it up. It is hard enough to do an event everyone loves, let alone one that has little support. Occasionally, you'll find an event that works year after year, and begins to have a life of its own. Encourage it and be grateful! Some events can become annual, anticipated, profitable events through a succession of leadership, both volunteer and staff.

When an event is over, the committee's work is not done. Each member should write down all the assignments completed, the suggestions for next time, and the cautions. The committee should get together a last time and talk through the entire event, taking notes and evaluating the project. No one will be able to remember, a year later, how many turkeys were needed to feed 275 people. Document everything. Next year's job will be easier, and you'll make more money.

Regardless of the event's success, do not allow your organization to rely too heavily on the proceeds. All it takes is one rainy summer weekend to create a year-long budget disaster, if you had counted on ticket sales for an outdoor event to meet your budget. Keep your annual fundraising activities diverse. Find ways to use the strengths of many different people, and find the maximum manageable ways to raise money in your community, given your capacity.

Most importantly, remember to thank your volunteers. In a smooth-running event, you may barely notice the hundreds of donated hours and the stressful decision-making that created your profit. To be sure, it was hard work. Almost nothing is as challenging as making money on volunteer events. Thank every volunteer, help your chair thank all the committees and helpers, and then help all the workers thank the chair. You can't do too much of it.

EVENT CONSULTANTS

It is hard work making money on special events, even when all the personnel time is donated. When you begin to consider hiring professional help, you are looking at multiplying your costs dramatically. You also may turn off some of your volunteer enthusiasm when a consultant is paid a major part of profits. Except in a large city, community feeling may be lost for an event that "goes professional."

When you hire professional help, you multiply your costs dramatically. You also may turn off some of your volunteer enthusiasm when a consultant is paid a large percentage of profits.

There are many event promoters around who will run a charitable event for your community and give you 15% to 30% of the profits afterward. You do no work at all. Organizations that choose this method, even at only 15% return, often say it is money they could not have raised on their own, and so something is better than nothing. That is a very short-range view. Keep in mind that your community is approached and asked to spend their money on a "charitable event," and they get the impression that they are making a charitable contribution. To find that only 15% to 30% of the ticket price is going to the charity is shocking. For the returns you will receive on the event, you'd be better off conducting a very modest event with volunteers and netting 85% of a smaller profit.

You can make good use of an events consultant if you use the person's expertise for planning and working with your volunteer leadership. This is much less costly than hiring someone to do all the work, but offers you the advantage of good advice and experience. Shop around for a consultant who has done your kind of event in the past, and interview carefully to make sure the consultant knows more than your experienced volunteers. Each community has a few people who are so good at running events that they could be events consultants themselves. Try to recruit them on your team!

GAMES OF CHANCE

Gambling is increasingly popular as a fundraising device, although it is just as quickly being outlawed in some states. The small local bingo games have grown, and in many cases are run by so-called "charitable" organizations, or by businesses that distribute some of the proceeds to nonprofits. In most cases, the percentage that makes its way back to the nonprofit is fairly small.

The other growing "charitable gambling" operation is the gambling hall for hire. Resorts or entertainment centers run an evening's gambling for a specific nonprofit, under contract, and a percentage of the evening's take goes to the nonprofit. The percentage will be small, after covering all costs and payment to the company, but the actual dollar return to the nonprofit may be large compared to proceeds from other fundraising projects. And there is no work involved.

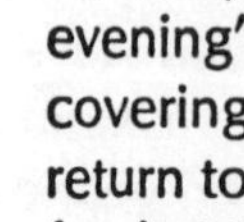

What you trade, rather than staff or volunteer time, in drawing your percentage, is image. While it will not hurt some organizations, a majority of nonprofits really cannot afford to have their public think that the budget is supported by gambling. Whether it is contrary to your specific mission or not, gambling is a questionable activity which is contrary to the ethics of much of our society. It is an activity that may be fine by personal choice, but is much more difficult to justify as a source of income for an organization chartered in the public trust.

It is a different matter if your volunteer team stages a one-night or weekend Casino Event for a fundraiser. When the event is run by volunteers and the funds, after modest and controlled expenses, all go to the nonprofit, you have a true charitable activity. Attendees know the greatest part of the money they spend goes to the cause. Middlemen are not taking profits. In this case, your group may decide Casino Night is fine. The sad thing is that the professional "casinos for charity" may turn the public away from the volunteer events that previously did quite well.

Before you enter any agreements to raise funds through an outside firm, meet with the promoters and read the contract carefully. Try out the idea on someone you trust outside your organization. Imagine the headlines the day after your event, and decide if you are comfortable with the outcome. Discuss it carefully with your volunteers, and discuss alternatives. Talk about the public image of your organization, what you would like it to become, and what your needs are. If it then seems like a good choice, go ahead, and good luck.

13 MEMBERSHIP RAISING

The key to understanding the membership drive is to see that it asks people to belong to something, unlike pure solicitation, which asks somebody to give.

A membership drive is not the same as an annual fund drive. Membership money is not the same as annual fund money. There are many similarities between membership and annual funds, starting with the fact that each is a yearly effort and including the fact that each brings in money. But the two are not synonymous and the distinctions are terribly important.

It is entirely possible for you to have a membership drive without having an annual fund drive or to have the annual fund drive without the membership drive. But, given the right circumstances, you will do the best for your organization if you have both.

The key to understanding the membership drive is to see that it asks people to *belong* to something, unlike pure solicitation, which asks somebody to *give*. Both are forms of support. The type of personal affiliation, and the individual's feeling of participation, are different.

Your members may not actually do anything different, but in giving their money for a membership appeal, they sense they are joining forces with you, putting their names on the line. In return, you will give them tangible benefits. These may be newsletters, gifts, discounts, or other special attention. In an annual fund drive, all you are offering in return for money is gratitude and, hopefully, the sight of your organization doing better. More importantly, gratitude is enough in an annual fund drive.

You will have many things to consider before you start a membership drive. Some of these questions are:

- Is this an appropriate organization for a membership appeal?
- How can we explain the membership so that it doesn't interfere with other fundraising?
- What benefits can we offer?
- What will it cost to service our members?
- Can we say membership fees are tax deductible as gifts?
- How can we make our membership augment our annual fund drive?
- What time of year will we invite people to become members?
- Will our members have governing privileges regarding the organization?

IS MEMBERSHIP APPROPRIATE?

Not all organizations are perfectly suited to having members. If your organization serves a broad part of the community, or if anybody might choose to participate in rather than "qualify for" participation, you may have a suitable membership organization. Museums, craft galleries, cultural organizations, public radio, public television, and community associations like arts councils, historical societies, and parent-teacher groups might all easily have memberships.

When you put the organization with good services together with the membership which has energy and warmth, the result is a fully involved organization with good utilization of people-power at all levels.

However, service and health organizations, educational institutions, and organizations to protect the homeless and disadvantaged may not be able to attract members. The reference to "membership" implies that people receive services from these organizations, which could be misleading. In those cases, the organization is best advised to establish a "Friends of...." organization, an auxiliary or a similar support group affiliated with the nonprofit.

While you want your membership organization to show real affiliation and support, you do not want to imply that your members receive selected services for their participation. As an example, a local mental health center could hardly ask for members, for it would give the impression that their members were receiving mental health counseling. But they could establish the Friends of the Town Mental Health Center, which would in turn have a membership, and those members would show support for the work of the Center.

Your first job is to decide how a membership operation might fit into your nonprofit. It will be particularly important for you to analyze this situation and fit your membership drive appropriately to your mission, because your membership is a great promotional device and ultimately brings new donors to your annual fund as well. It is important that your membership accurately represent the people who are affiliated with you and your partnership with them.

EXPLAINING MEMBERSHIP

Communication is crucial. At no time do you want your members to feel that they have already made an annual contribution to the organization through their membership fees. Many organizations get into trouble with this, either because they don't explain it well, or because they impose an annual fund on top of a membership drive without planning, explaining and appropriately timing it.

You can avoid difficulties and keep a very happy membership, and at the same time have a large percentage of your members donating to the annual fund of your organization. But the only way to do this is to be absolutely clear about the purposes of these two separate drives.

You must stress to your members that the annual fund pays for the operations of the organization. It is a renewable fund, for which they will be solicited every year, and which covers the costs of salaries, utilities, outreach and basic operations. The membership, while it is supportive of the organization, is directed at the members themselves. It's a form of communication, goodwill and cooperation. It draws the members closer to the organization and allows them input in your planning and your accomplishment of goals.

Imagine an organization that has no membership, but has an effective annual fund. It goes about its business in a cool way, providing needed services but with a sense of distance to the community. Now imagine a membership without a mission. You have a social club, an opportunity for people to meet each other and develop friendships, and a pooling of undirected energies. Each of these is only half the perfect equation. When you put the organization with good services together with the membership which has energy and warmth, the result is a fully involved organization with good utilization of people power at all levels.

MEMBER BENEFITS

Once you've decided how memberships will fit with the rest of your operation, you need to explore the benefits that you might be able to offer. Your basic choices are tangible or intangible gifts, and publications. All these will cost you money, and you should approach this issue in a businesslike way. Your goal should be to provide the most attractive benefits to your members at the lowest possible cost to your organization.

Your membership gift will whisper your name to a member repeatedly.

You need to find benefits that you will be able to sustain or augment over a long period of time, and which will have a retained value for your members. Remember, not all people give to a membership drive out of purely philanthropic intent. Many people will become members in order to give you a little support and get your special offer in return. That's all right, so long as you start working immediately to create charitable interest in that member for your future membership and annual fund drives.

On the other hand, you are not becoming a retail operation and you have no obligation to become a benefit vendor. If you want to offer benefits, find the ones that will help the person who is on the fence make the decision to join.

Tangible Benefits

Tangible membership benefits are usually gifts, such as a tee-shirt, a hat, a mug, a tote bag, note cards, an umbrella or any other useful, small item that can be mailed inexpensively. This is good public relations, and most people find it inoffensive and, sometimes, fun. Current IRS rulings (as of this writing) encourage this, with no declaration necessary for benefits worth less than $5.50 and for those with logos or other insignia. (Tax deductibility is discussed in greater detail later in this chapter.)

Be aware of the fact that your membership gift will, in a sense, whisper your name to your member repeatedly. Represent yourself the way you would choose to be remembered. For instance, if you are an organization advocating to save the rain forests, you would probably give a bad message if your membership gift was a small tropical plant for people to keep in their homes. You could argue that the tropical plant had been grown in a florist shop and was only symbolic, but it could be perceived as an abuse of natural systems, and that you were promoting an unnatural environment for tropical plants. Similarly, if you are a society for the advancement of American music, don't offer a cassette recording of Brahms or Ravel as a benefit, not even if the local record store gave you a carton of them for free! Remember that your gift carries your message; it's another form of "putting your money where your mouth is!"

Intangible Benefits

Intangible membership benefits include discounts on purchases, free admissions or discounted series tickets to events. Like a tote bag printed with your logo, an intangible membership benefit repeats your name to supporters year-round and makes them feel part of a special club. You may be able to provide your members with something they cannot get anywhere else.

These benefits may be very attractive at budget time because they don't require a cash investment, but they may have an impact on your revenue later. If you have a limited number of seats to sell and are counting on selling a certain number to break even, an influx of membership discounts could wreck your budget. You also will feel real hesitation to turn away subscribers or ticket holders who may have far greater potential to help you financially. So, you must be careful even in giving intangibles.

Another intangible benefit is voting rights at your annual meeting. This is the cheapest benefit, financially, and the most expensive in all other terms. Consider it carefully. You have to be certain that you are entrusting the future of your organization to those people who really should be making decisions. You must also be certain you have the staff capacity to work with a voting membership, including notification for meetings, conducting annual membership events, and the "hassle factor" of hundreds of opinions halting your work.

Publications

The third category of membership benefits is one that serves both you and the donor but requires a great deal of work on your part: publications. There is hardly a better way for you to communicate your activities and health as an organization to a vast cross section of your community than through the printed word.

A newsletter is a wonderful membership benefit. In fact, you don't even want your members to have the opportunity to refuse the newsletter, as it is such a good promotional device. But to produce such a document on a regular basis, and to send it to a large number of people, you must be prepared to invest staff time in organization, writing, editing and producing a document that truly represents the quality of your organization. This, and other publications, offers you almost unlimited exposure with great internal control.

As important as it is, do not allow your newsletter or magazine to overtake delivery of basic services.

As important as it is, do not allow your newsletter or magazine to overtake delivery of basic services. If you cannot afford a staff person to do a good job, investigate the possibility of using some of your volunteers or members to produce the newsletter. Consider contracting with freelancers. But whatever you do, assure yourself that the quality will be on a level with the quality of services you offer in your field. You cannot afford to have a top-notch organization represented to the public with a sloppy or illiterate news document; you also do not want to have a fine, comprehensive and beautiful document reporting the demise of the organization.

THE COSTS OF SERVICING MEMBERS

It is really distressing to observe nonprofit perceptions of membership money. For one thing, many nonprofits view all the membership money that comes in as gift money. They lump together 100% of the membership proceeds and plug it into the annual fund revenue line on their budget. They try to believe that all the money that comes in from members is contributions and available for operations expense.

On the other hand, they develop benefit packages for members with little regard to the expense involved. It is not unusual to find an organization that is providing each member with 10% to 50% more benefit value than the actual membership fee. Shockingly, it is sometimes these very same organizations that are considering membership income as contribution money. This leads to a very dangerous situation.

You must approach your membership appeal as a business venture. If you determine that some of your membership income will be fed into the annual fund, you must take that money off the top. It is not necessary to do this, and you may have very good reasons for investing 100% of your membership income in direct benefits to the members, but that must be a conscious decision and you must be aware of the implications that it has for your organization.

A good rule of thumb for a benefit item would be to offer combined benefits that would cost no more than one quarter of the membership fee.

It may be very expensive for you to attract new members for their first and second years. This is typical; it may cost as much or more than the membership fee to identify, attract and service your new members. This may be responsible, depending upon your reasons for wanting a membership, if you can project a fairly good retention level after year two.

As you review the possibilities for benefits, explore all of the costs involved. If you select a mug, you must look at the purchase price of the item, the cost of printing it with your logo, the cost of the packaging, the postage expense, and the contingency costs of breakage, surplus, and storage of inventory. Not only that, you have to consider the hidden costs of staff or volunteer time and organization in ordering, packing, addressing and otherwise handling the mug. You can't just shrug your shoulders and say, "We'll all just pack them in our spare time," because doing that can eat up everybody's time and prevent you from completing other tasks.

You also need to consider the retail value of your gift, were it available in retail stores, and the psychological impact of that comparable value in relationship to the membership costs. You do not want your benefit to be too excessive in comparison to membership fees. Your members could be offended at your money management or your extravagance. In considering retail value, do not consider the fact that your gift item may be donated to you. Even if you tell your members that the gift was donated, they will not factor that into their psychological reaction to the gift.

A good rule of thumb for a benefit item would be to offer combined benefits that would, at retail, cost no more than one quarter of the membership fee. Therefore, someone paying a $40 membership fee might receive an item that would have approximately a $5 retail value, plus newsletters or other publications. Five to ten additional dollars will be spent on related expenses, as the following example shows:

- If you were to spend $5 to purchase a mug that might sell at $9.95 retail as a tangible benefit for a $40 member, you would also have to figure into your expenses the cost of packing materials and postage, about $2.50, and staff or volunteer time to prepare the items for mailing, another $1.50 per item. Meanwhile, you will have some miscellaneous costs for imprinting your logo and printing any promotional materials, which might add another dollar to the handling costs of the mug. Therefore, you are spending $5 of your own money in addition to the $5 purchase price for the mug, and your $40 member is costing you $10 in service. This is entirely outside the cost of retaining the member's participation.

In sum, your consideration of the cost of a benefit must be comprehensive and must provide you with an expense that is significantly lower than the membership fee. Continuing with the previous example, if you are providing a mug to our $40 member at a benefit cost of $10 to the organization, you may also be sending a newsletter four times a year and sending membership renewals at least once a year. Those costs will probably add up to another $5-$10 per member. Thus, out of a $40 membership fee, this imaginary organization will realize, at best, $20-$25 of that as a direct contribution to the organization. This is an excellent scenerio and leaves this organization in far better shape than most membership organizations.

If you find your projected membership benefit expenses creeping up to 75% or higher, stop and rethink the situation. With the possibility of cost overruns, low response leaving inventory, and the unpredictability of a membership drive in general, anything less than 25% projected profit on a membership drive is really dangerous. You could easily find yourself subsidizing your membership drive with operational funds, which would quickly weaken your organization.

ARE MEMBERSHIP FEES TAX DEDUCTIBLE?

Membership fees are not always tax deductible to their full dollar amount, and you must be cautious in promising deductibility to your donors. The question revolves around benefits.

If you offer a tangible benefit worth less than $5.50, your donor can still consider the membership fee a contribution. If the benefit item is higher, the value of the gift must be subtracted from the membership fee to determine the tax-deductible amount. If members buy a ticket to attend a dinner or other event, that cost may cut the deductible amount. It is your obligation to inform the donor of the gift value. However, if you simply invite the member to a dinner not tied to benefits, the entire membership stays tax deductible.

If your benefits include newsletters or magazines that promote your organization, those do not have a dollar value in figuring deductions. Nor do voting rights or the other intangible benefits that a member may or may not choose to exercise.

HOW THE MEMBERSHIP DRIVE AUGMENTS THE ANNUAL FUND

Members do prospect research for you by identifying themselves as potential annual fund donors, potential volunteers and potential board members.

A great challenge in running a good membership drive is to see membership as a tool toward a more effective annual fund. Remember that annual fund gifts are 100% devoted to operational expenses, whereas membership fees may only yield you 25% to 50% for operational expenses; you can see that every dollar that comes into the annual fund is more valuable to your operation than your membership drive. However, your membership drive is one of your great development tools and ultimately builds your fund.

Members do prospect research for you by identifying themselves as potential annual fund donors, potential volunteers and potential board members. Your members do you a service each time they join, simply because they are signaling to you that their interest is continuing and they like the way you are operating.

Your members may also be more willing to suggest their friends as potential members than as potential donors. Being a member is much more participatory than being a donor, and it is more attractive to many people. Do remember, though, that there are some people who would like just to give you an annual fund contribution and forget about the membership. Some people are not joiners. If you keep both drives going, you'll find that a majority of your members will also be annual fund donors, some members will not give to the annual fund, and some annual fund donors will not become members.

Membership gives you the opportunity to solicit opinions and to thank your donors in a variety of ways. It provides a social contact for thanking your helpers and donors and for drawing people into the auxillary services of your organization. And the activities of your members will attract the kind of newspaper publicity that you cannot get on a repeated basis when you only feature your operations and services.

Typically today, it costs a great deal to attract new members. National organizations assume that two to four years of membership fees will be entirely consumed in the expense of initially attracting each donor.

However, those same donors may become annual fund donors as early as year one. For instance, an organization may spend $25 to $45 in year one attracting a $25 membership. In year two, soliciting renewal of that membership may cost $10. However, when year three comes, it may cost only $1.25 to bring that member back into the fold. Once the third-year membership has been achieved, that member is fairly well established, and may stick with the organization for ten years or more.

Meanwhile, the same donor may make a contribution of $10 to the annual fund in the first year. The solicitation expense may have been $2 for that $10 gift. In year two, the annual fund gift may go up to $20, and it still is costing the organization only $2 to solicit the gift. In year 3, the annual fund gift is likely to go up and the membership is paying off. By the third year, the member is providing operational money through the annual fund and through the membership drive, and may actively be helping the organization in other ways as well.

Look at your membership appeal as an overall expense of the organization and as a long-term building operation. It is important for you and your board to recognize the fact that new members are expensive to attract, but that old members make up the difference.

WHEN TO CONDUCT THE MEMBERSHIP DRIVE

Donors are creatures of habit, and therefore any effort to revamp their "giving calendar" should be considered with care. In any new fundraising effort, you should make your current, effective fundraising programs take precedence. You can change those habits, but do it in a way that will increase your donations, not destabilize them.

Before you decide when to conduct your membership drive, you need to make a few other decisions.

- When will you conduct your annual fund drive?
- How many solicitations will you make?
- Who will do the work of the membership appeal?
- Will the membership drive be during a short time, or all year long?

If volunteers will send out membership materials, keep the records and acknowledge returns, you may want to have an "anniversary" system membership: each person has a renewal date, and the drive goes on year-round. On the other hand, if this will be a staff activity, it might be best to do it all at one time and get it over with.

The single renewal date method makes it very clear to your members that there is a specific time of year for renewal. If they are late to pay, it is their loss, not yours. It also makes it easier to publicize the membership drive, which is hardly newsworthy when it runs all year long. An organization with a fiscal year of July 1 through June 30 might conduct an annual fund drive with solicitations in September and November and a reminder in May. During the lull at mid-year, January, the membership drive can be conducted with great energy. Not only is this a slow time for the annual appeal, it is a very logical time to solicit calendar-year memberships for the organization.

Donors are creatures of habit, and therefore any effort to revamp their "giving calendar" should be considered with care.

There's a bonus in this for you. If you can organize your volunteers to work extra hard in January to solicit memberships, you'll have their other 11 months of the year for other kinds of work, such as special events and annual fund assistance, and public relations or programmatic assistance. Whereas, spreading a little bit of volunteer energy over the whole year exhausts some of your best helpers on just one task, year after year. They can get bored that way, and you may lose them after a short time.

If you have the energy, time and postage money to spend, you can augment your membership drive by reminding people in December that their memberships will be expiring in a month. You can ask them to save you some expense and send their memberships right away, accelerating their tax deduction and your income. For those who do not renew or join in January, you can send a reminder in February and tell them what benefits they will be losing if they do not rejoin for the year.

Memberships are traditionally for one year. Some organizations offer life memberships, at high prices, but they eventually decide that it does not pay off. People seldom write checks to nonprofits for more than they can currently afford, so people who pay high rates for life membership could usually write a check for that amount every year. They could certainly afford to pay low membership rates year after year and make increasingly larger gifts to the annual fund. Writing a check for a high-cost lifetime membership sticks in the donor's mind as a great generosity, so the donor may feel it replaces an annual gift for several years.

SHOULD YOU OFFER GOVERNING PRIVILEGES?

Up to this point we have been concentrating on memberships in a nonlegalistic sense. But in fact there are two different interpretations of membership organizations, and you must discover which one applies to you.

If your by-laws define you as a membership organization with a voting membership, annual meetings and governance rights, you will be directed by the voting action of your members.

On the other hand, if you are a nonprofit directed by a board of directors, with no reference in the by-laws to a voting membership, you can still conduct a "membership appeal" to solicit funds and help you garner supporters. You can still call these people "members," yet not offer governing privileges. This, of course, is far less difficult to manage than the governing membership.

Regardless of the cost of membership and the cost of the benefits, your people get far more than their dollars' worth. They get the sense of participation and helpfulness in an organization that shares their personal beliefs, and that is worth more than money. They get a chance to make a difference.

If your organization is looking for real grass-roots participation, and if you want your board of directors to be elected by a membership rather than appointed by a self-perpetuating board, then you will need a governing membership. Depending upon the type of organization you are, and upon your mission, this may help you in public relations, in longevity of the organization and in public representation. It will probably not help you very much in fundraising.

If you want to be governed by a board of directors and if you expect them to perpetuate themselves with appointments to the board, and if you expect your fundraising to be done in great part by the board, you may not want to have a general membership that votes. If you want to be able to take quick action, hold private meetings, or set and follow a long-range plan without repeated interference, then you are better off without a voting membership. This single question can determine much of the style, image and accessibility of your organization.

Whichever kind of a membership you choose, you should conduct a membership drive and charge a membership fee. Remember that membership means benefits, and benefits mean expenses. Regardless of the cost of membership and the cost of the benefits, your people get far more than their dollars' worth. They get the sense of participation and helpfulness in an organization that shares their personal beliefs, and that is worth more than money. They get a chance to make a difference.

In fact, that is the very reason that you will be able to solicit your members for annual fund gifts above and beyond your membership fees. There really is room for both techniques as means of generating money, volunteers, energy and personal support.

14 WHAT ANNUAL FUNDS ARE NOT

By this time, you may be feeling that "annual fund" is a term synonomous with "fundraising." Actually, the annual fund is a field within fundraising which exemplifies the rules and methods of all other types of campaigns. However, there are several types of fundraising and drives which are not appropriate for your annual campaign. These should be avoided, not because they will not generate funds but because they take too long, produce restricted gifts, or will eat up your time without annual pay-off.

Keep in mind, as you plan your annual drive and as you implement the plan, that the annual fund pays for operations on a yearly basis. It is a fund that must be raised anew every year. It must be unrestricted money that can be spent on the essentials of day-to-day operation. If you think of a questionable way to raise money ask yourselves these questions:

- Can we use the proceeds to pay the phone bill?
- Can we solicit these donors again next year?
- Will this activity help us gain new, repeating, donors?

We all have a tendency to be attracted to the "greener grass" of new types of fundraising. If you've been busily soliciting for the annual campaign, the thought of talking to donors about something jazzier than operating expenses will often be appealing. Don't give in! You've got to have a steadfast, solid, even dogged approach to the annual fund. When the time is right, you can consider these other methods and do good planning to integrate them into your overall fundraising plan. Till the time is right, avoid them and avoid confusion.

CAPITAL CAMPAIGNS

Capital campaigns are major fund drives conducted for a short, predetermined length of time, for a specific purpose. While they used to be primarily for building construction, capital campaigns are now commonly used for major renovations, endowment funds, scholarship drives, acquistion funds, and for investment in major organizational change. Depending upon the need and your track record, you might be able to raise 10 to 50 times your annual fund total in a capital drive, over a period of two to five years, with pledge payments spread over the same period of time.

The temptation of the capital drive is the enormity of the funds you may be able to raise. Faced with a constantly draining annual fund, you may see a big, one-time campaign as the answer to your prayers. But you must remember that donors will only give to such a drive if there's good reason. And that usually means a big-ticket item that you can purchase or pay for in one shot. While you may think that a shrinking annual fund is good reason to conduct a capital campaign, your donors will be hard to convince. In fact, if your annual fund needs help, your capital campaign is in trouble from the start.

While you may think that a shrinking annual fund is good reason to conduct a capital campaign, your donors will be hard to convince. In fact, if your annual fund needs help, your capital campaign is in trouble from the start.

If you need a capital campaign to bolster your organization and your annual fund, then you need more basic help than pledges. A capital campaign is for a healthy organization. Backtrack a few steps and start reviewing your mission, your budget, your goals and your fundraising plans. You cannot use a capital campaign solely to stabilize your organization, and you cannot use even a portion of it if the gifts have been restricted to another purpose. You may need deep and thorough reassessment.

ENDOWMENT DRIVES

An endowment is often created through a capital campaign, but some organizations develop a special short-term fundraising effort specially to set aside an endowment. The theory of endowment is that invested principal will generate interest income annually which can be used to pay the bills. The principal provides a cushion for hard times. This was a good argument in the past, and still works for larger organizations as part of a major capital campaign.

For community organizations, this is a very tough idea to sell. In the days when donors had their own personal endowments, when most donors were of the wealthiest part of society, this idea made a lot of sense. They wanted their pet causes to have the same financial security they provided for their own families. But today, our donors represent all parts of society, and very few of them have family endowments. They perceive an endowment search as a luxury, something they wish they had and you wish you had, but not very likely for either of you.

If you have a true capital campaign at some time in the future, earmark some of the funds for endowment and you'll acheive a bit of security. For the time being, spending your time working for the type of gifts that might contribute to endowment will be contrary to your annual needs unless you have enough staff to allow someone to concentrate on endowment. And the small percentage of income you may accumulate each year during the earlier stages of the fund will not justify the staff and volunteer investment you will make; wait till you can afford to do it right.

When you do establish an endowment, it will not produce a windfall for your annual expenses unless it is extraordinarily large. You might reasonably count on 5%, hopefully just a portion of the income, to add to your operating budget. In keeping with traditional endowment management, your advisors will probably require that you reinvest a healthy portion of the endowment income annually in order to grow the fund and keep up with inflation. This considered, the annual fund may have very little to gain from your enormous efforts to start an endowment if you have to develop a campaign and solicit the funds.

BEQUESTS

This is another area of great fundraising potential that is simply inappropriate for a tightly scheduled annual fund office. To do an effective job in the bequests area, you must identify prospects carefully and cultivate them over a long period of time. You may have no idea of the effectiveness of your solicitation until after your prospect has died, and even then you may have to wait through a long estate probate to receive the funds. You do need this kind of gift, but you cannot afford to use your annual fund time and energy to work on it.

Make it clear, in all your printed materials, that you are delighted to discuss and accept bequests. Then let fate take its course.

The best compromise concerning bequests is probably this: make it clear, in all your printed materials, that you are delighted to discuss and accept bequests. Ascertain with legal counsel your ability to accept such gifts. Then let fate take its course, or turn this over to the planned giving specialist in your organization, or do it yourself when you have completed all your annual fund work.

Very often, donors of bequests limit the options for use of the income from their gifts. The annual fund may not be high on the list. This makes it all the more inappropriate for your energy and efforts.

If you've done a fine cultivation job in your annual fund, you may very well receive some bequests. It takes a long time. Don't stew about it, and don't feel disappointed if they don't come through. If you do a spectacular annual fundraising job, maybe someday you can afford to hire a planned gifts officer to invest real time in this area, and then things will begin to happen. Meanwhile, luck and good fortune may come your way.

PLANNED GIFTS

There are other planned gifts in addition to bequests, and they are a bit less risky but no less time consuming. Unlike an anticipated or promised bequest, the terms of which can be changed by the donor at any time during his or her life without your knowledge, gifts of trusts, tangible property, and real estate can be negotiated and consummated while your donor lives to enjoy your appreciation (and, probably, significant tax benefits too).

But these gifts still take a great deal of time and require skills that a typical annual fund office may not have. The immediate cash rewards may not be great either, as the income from a trust may go to the donor for many years before you receive the principal. If you receive the income, it may be designated for restricted purposes. Because these are usually major gifts, your donor may want to restrict the use of principal for a pet project as well, making the planned gift even more of a risk for your annual fund operation. Keep your job description and organizational needs clearly in mind before you begin to spend your time on these gifts.

GRANTS AND SPECIAL DRIVES

Grants have a way of disappearing just as you become dependent upon them.

Two borderline efforts, which may or may not be appropriate for your annual fund drive, are grants and special drives. If your budget has been inflated by a special need such as a new project start-up or a new piece of equipment, it may be necessary to attempt to raise substantially increased funds to cover those costs in one year's time. If that is so, obtaining a grant or conducting a short, restricted drive may be a good way to fulfill budget needs.

If your budget is creeping up and probably will stay up, you need a long-lasting method of paying for new expenses, and grants or special drives simply will not provide you with a long-term answer.

Think of grants as project money, start-up money, and one-time investments. Think of special drives as very short-term influxes of cash that may buy you equipment, such as computer systems. In this way, you can keep your organization stable and maintain a healthy annual fund that will continue to pay for operational costs.

Do not become reliant on grants and special drives. Grants have a way of disappearing just as you become dependent upon them. Special drives have a way of becoming crisis calls for repairing budgetary shortfalls. Neither are safe ways to fund your organization for the long haul.

Section Four ■ Your Fundraising Support System

Annual funds are not reinvented each year, they are refined. This theory works because you accumulate repeating donors. They repeat because they feel appreciated and needed. Making them feel that way is your greatest responsibility.

15 SAYING THANKS

For all the hard work you invest in fundraising, one would think you'd be deeply appreciative when the money comes in. And you are. But it is remarkable how many omissions, delays and neglects occur in thanking donors.

Nothing is more important than saying thank you. You should do it promptly, from the heart, and repeatedly. You cannot err by thanking somebody too much, but you can cause irreversible damage by thanking too little.

Nothing is more important than saying thank you. You should do it promptly, from the heart, and repeatedly.

Regardless of the size of the gift, a thank-you note or card absolutely must go to the donor within days. The optimum turnaround time is one day, but if you cannot manage that, be absolutely certain to get the thank you out within the same week that you received the gift. A carbon receipt is not a suitable thank you, even if the alternative is a printed card. Send the card, and, if possible, have a person sign it. It is much more appreciative.

Do not rely on volunteers who stop in every two weeks, or once a month, to write thank-you notes. If you have to wait that long for their help, do the notes yourself. Later, volunteers can write second thank-you notes to reinforce your appreciation.

Not only is it absolutely important to say thanks quickly, but your donor needs to know that you've received the check. It is important that the check clears the account quickly. There is hardly anything as distressing as a phone call from a donor, much later, asking if you'd ever received a check. If you find the uncashed check in a pile on your desk, you'll be mortified. Don't let it happen to you.

For some reason, frantic gift officers concentrate more on the money still to be raised than on the money that comes in. There is a tendency to take our donors for granted once they send in the check, while we bestow heaps of attention on potential donors. This is crazy, but it

If you recognize your donors' generosity with a pure spirit, you'll find your work becomes easier, more pleasant and more gratifying as well as more successful.

happens all the time. The same thing goes for foundations, corporations and other sources of funding. Your donors are your best friends, and you need to tell them that, and keep it that way. You can only do that by showing appreciation.

Tailor the nature of your thank you to the nature of the solicitation. If a gift comes in response to an impersonal, direct mail piece, a printed thank you is perfectly sufficient. If the solicitation was personalized with a real signature, the thank-you card can be improved with a personal signature and a few hand-written words on the printed note.

Similarly, a gift that comes in response to a face-to-face solicitation by a volunteer, even if it does not live up to your hopes, should be thanked with a personal word plus the printed acknowledgment. Always let your solicitors know the outcome of their work. When a contribution comes in that has been requested by a volunteer, send the official appreciation from the office; then send a photocopy to or phone the involved volunteers to let them know about the gift so they can send their own personal note. Don't assume that your volunteer will think of doing this; supply some note paper as a reminder that thank yous should be written promptly and easily.

Some organizations have had stamps made for endorsing the backs of checks which say, "Thank you for your contribution to XYZ," naming their organization. While this is a nice added touch, it in no way takes the place of a real thank you. The number of people who actually look at the back of their checks for endorsements is miniscule, and in any case, it is far too impersonal to be a real sign of appreciation. Remember too, that *recognition* goes beyond a thank-you note or other specific thanks. Your best donors, and those climbing to the ranks of best donors, need other kinds of recognition. The most obvious is to name something for the donor; other simpler forms include prominent listings of donors in your lobby, listings in your annual report, words of gratitude at a speech or event, an occasional note or phone call simply to say hello, and any of many other thoughtful, kind signs of appreciation. Try to recognize your donor, in a variety of ways, several times before you ask for another gift. If you recognize your donors' generosity with a pure spirit, you'll find your work becomes easier, more pleasant and more gratifying as well as more successful.

When a donor requests anonymity, you must respect that choice totally. Nothing kills a donor's generosity faster than the organization's mishandling of recognition. But remember, even the most private donor, requesting total anonymity, wants to know you appreciated the gift. You simply must be more creative and sensitive in finding ways to recognize the giver. Don't be afraid to discuss this with a major donor; perhaps through shared conversation you two can come up with an appropriate and gracious way to recognize a gift without pointing a finger at the donor. But even in cases of smaller gifts, always show your appreciation to the donor, no matter how private that expression must be.It is well worth checking and double-checking your thank-you mechanisms regularly. This is far too often neglected, and the results are only discovered much later when gifts fall off, volunteers drop out, or feelings of unhappiness about the organization begin to emerge. You can do a great deal to keep your giving program at a high and enthusiastic level by saying a simple thank you.

16 KEEPING ENERGY HIGH

Remember to thank your volunteers as well. Remember that a good volunteer's time is in demand, and the assignments require courage and determination. No matter how much they like your organization, their investment of time and energy is crucial to you and must be acknowledged.

After a solicitation is completed, even if you have a written call report in hand, call your volunteer, thank him or her, and ask how things went. Don't postpone this! It's not only a good opportunity for you to take some notes on the conversation and outcome as the volunteer describes them, but also, more importantly, it's an opportunity for you to tell the volunteer how much you appreciate the work.

Get to know your volunteers. Listen to them. Be a partner.

If your volunteers are involved in a long project, give them frequent encouragement and express your appreciation often. If your volunteers are busy, you are probably doubly busy and this may be the last thing on your mind, but it really will keep them going.

Use your imagination in thanking your volunteers. While you don't want to spend hard raised money on presents, a token gift is often doubly appreciated by a volunteer, for its unexpectedness and its kindness. You may be able to offer a convenience, a service, or some odd thing which is easy for your organization but hard otherwise to come by. Use of space at your facility after hours might be valuable to a volunteer, or use of your computer, copier, piano, kitchen or coffee urns. Use your imagination!

At the end of a project, do give your volunteers recognition. Give a party or a dinner. Consider having staff do all the work. This can be an opportunity for announcing accomplished goals, promoting new projects, or whatever is appropriate, but be sure to keep the volunteers and their recognition first on the agenda.

Budget a little something in your development expense to make sure that you can pull this off. A sign of personal appreciation is wonderful. Make sure also that your chief volunteers or team leaders understand your policy about showing appreciation, and that they thank the volunteers who work for and with them.

Sometimes we begin to feel guilty about asking so much of our volunteers. Guilt can devastate your efforts to get the work done.

One of the best ways to keep the energy level high and stay excited about the work is through regular updates on progress.

Remember that your volunteer is involved because of personal commitment, and wants to see success too! You do need to be aware of your volunteer's personal situation. Some people cannot say no, and you will occasionally need to give a volunteer a break. But don't do it for the wrong reasons; do it because you have listened, and know the volunteer needs it.

You can avoid burn-out and stress by doing adequate planning for your fundraising. Never place the volunteer in the position of soliciting in a short timeframe because you didn't plan far enough in advance. With enough time, fundraising can be done in a comfortable, informal way, and your volunteers can feel good about their work.

One of the best ways to keep the energy level high and stay excited about the work is through regular updates on progress. Make oral reports at board meetings, and send reports if you meet infrequently. A sample format is shown in Figure 17.

Use your own judgment about comparative results on individual assignments. Some groups and volunteers thrive on competition, and others wilt in the face of it. Assess your helpers and their personalities, and report accordingly. Plain embarrassment may chase away the slower volunteers.

You'll do much better at fundraising if you like people, enjoy personal relationships and have a natural tendency to take care of other people's needs. If this is hard for you, be mindful of it and challenge yourself. All fundraising succeeds because people make contact with each other and share dreams, energy and excitment.

Keep one eye on your businesslike plans and the other eye on your people. Allow yourself to have fun and make your fundraising time human. Send birthday cards and wedding gifts, surprise people, call just to say hello, and offer sympathy when appropriate. Get to know your volunteers. Listen to them. Be a partner. Always be the first to remember WHY you are all working together: for the mission, not for your job. Loosen up and have a good time!

Figure 17: Annual Fund Progress Report

Date ____________________

Amount of time since Kick-Off (November 15) ______________

Number of personal solicitations completed ________________

Number of personal solicitations pending _________________

Board members who have completed solicitation assignments:

____

____

____

____

____

____

____

Total dollars in personal solicitation to date: _________

Total dollars in board contributions to date: _________

Total dollars in mail solicitations to date: _________

Total annual appeal to date: _________

If you need more information to complete your assignments, please call us at (phone) any day!

17 COMMON AVOIDANCE TECHNIQUES AND CURES

At first, people do not usually have good feelings about fundraising assignments. Like kids with homework, board members can find a million reasons not to do their solicitations. Fundraising is a challenging assignment but it is not so terrible that it deserves all this avoidance. It is the myriad psychological aspects that make people cringe.

Anybody who has spent time in development offices knows the signs of avoidance well. As staff or board fundraising chairperson, your task is to learn how to counteract these hesitations and help your board members discover for themselves the pride and excitement of raising money for a good cause.

Following is a sampling of all-time winning avoidance techniques and the answers you need to know to help your board be more effective.

- ***"I'll do anything except raise money."***

This is like saying, "I'll do anything except make certain this organization can survive." When you join a board, you are making a statement that you truly share the philosophy of the organization, and you believe it deserves to survive. If you are willing to invest your time and your money in its future, you must be willing to do the necessary tasks. There are only two basic jobs of the board of any organization: to set policy, and to assure financial viability. No board member should be able to pick one or the other. Both are crucial. And in a nonprofit, raising money is essential to financial viability.

- ***"I give my time, that should be enough."***

Both time and money are essential. One without the other simply is not enough. If you give time, you are a volunteer. If you give money, you are a donor. Both are essential. But if you are a board member, you must give time and money. Time and money go hand-in-hand. If you want to do less, the board is not the place for you.

■ ***"The fundraising committee ought to do the fundraising."***

The fundraising committee would be given an unfair burden if that minority of the board was held responsible for balancing the budget with contributions. It is the fundraising committee's responsibility to develop or approve a reasonable fundraising plan, in partnership with staff. That plan should be brought to the board for full approval. Then board members must all pitch in and help raise the funds in the manner spelled out in the plan.

These questions can often be resolved by returning to the basic board responsibilities: setting policy and assuring financial stability. Those tasks are crucial enough that all board members must cooperate toward achieving them.

■ ***"I have a conflict of interest, so I can't ask for money."***

What are you doing on the board with that substantial conflict of interest? The board is the ultimate support group for any organization: it is the family, the place where secrets and fears are shared. There is no room on the board for a person who can step back and declare exemption.

Talk seriously with potential board members before they join; often the people we want most are the ones who have already made a commitment to a similar cause. Make certain that your board members can support you wholeheartedly. Board members can serve on two related boards and raise money for both organizations; this is not an impossible situation unless the member finds it untenable. If that is the case, ask for a leave of absence or resignation.

Someone who makes an intense personal effort, even a sacrifice, to make a $100 gift may be the perfect solicitor for your $1000 prospect.

Most often, the plea of "conflict of interest" is a sign that the board member is uncomfortable with fundraising in general. The conflict can easily be worked through. Listen carefully, and if this seems to be the case, gently attempt to teach that board member solicitation skills. If the problem simply is that the board member is not convinced about the organization, educate him or her more thoroughly; if it still doesn't work, the member probably should leave the board.

■ ***"I don't know the right people."***

Obviously, some of the "right people" are those with a great deal of money to give away. But the "right people" are also those who share your beliefs, who think your organization is important and deserves to thrive, who want to help in whatever way they can. Every one of your board members knows some of the right people, and you can help discover who they are. Your board members can help you make more people "right" for your cause.

Big gifts are wonderful, but they are not the only gifts. More than half the money donated by individuals in the United States every year comes from people who make less than $30,000 in household income. If you were determined to do so, you could meet your goal every year with gifts of $100 and under.

It's a lot less work to bring in some larger gifts too, and that's what you aim to do. But your board members can help you at all levels

■ ***"I can't give much myself, so I can't ask."***

Tradition says that people should ask their peers for gifts, that big

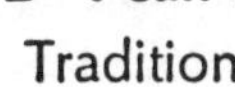

donors should ask for big gifts, that $1000 donors should solicit other $1000 donors. But there has to be another way. In small communities, rural areas and in some grassroots organizations, it will be impossible to find enough board members capable of giving large gifts to solicit the potential major donors identified.

The key thing in this situation is commitment. Someone who makes an intense personal effort, even a sacrifice, to make a $100 gift may be the perfect solicitor for your $1000 prospect. Sincerity is unmistakable in solicitation. Your prospect will be convinced by a highly committed donor who can truly say, "I believe deeply in this work, and I have made the largest gift I can afford. My resources are not as great as some, but I have done my best. It's my greatest hope that you'll join me with a serious commitment to our cause, with a gift of $1000."

Remember our question of knowing the right people? The "right people" are the people who believe in your work, and the right solicitors are the ones who can express that in words. If you have those "right" people on your board, the money will follow.

- ***"No one told me I'd have to raise money on this board."***

Someone was not doing a good job, if this is the case. When someone is asked onto your board, you must spell out the job. You, or the nominating committee, must describe all the board responsibilities with frankness and thoroughness. It is unfair to your potential board member and ultimately unfair to the organization to promise that the job will be easy, that meetings are optional or infrequent, that there's really nothing to do, or that anyone will be exempt from fundraising.

Remind yourself and your board members that you are not asking for money for yourselves. When solicitation focuses on the cause rather than the people, it gains dignity.

- ***"I like being on the board, but there's something belittling about fundraising."***

It's more likely that the solicitor feels incompetent because she or he hasn't had enough training, doesn't have enough information about the organization, or has been matched with prospects with whom she or he feels uncomfortable. Fundraising is a learned skill, and each board member should have the opportunity to learn how to do it well. You can help by arranging for training sessions in solicitation and by offering thoughtful suggestions. Many courageous veteran fundraisers even go so far as to call fundraising a noble pursuit because it enables us to improve our world.

Remind yourself and your board members that you are not asking for money for yourselves. When solicitation focuses on the cause rather than the people, it gains dignity.

- ***"Fundraising? That's what we hired the development person for!"***

The most effective solicitors will always be the volunteers, the people who give of their time because they so strongly believe in the organization and its goals.

A good development officer is an incredible asset: a helper who can gather important research, help identify prospects, set goals, suggest fundraising methods, offer training, establish good records, develop effective written materials, make appointments, and even accompany a board member on a solicitation call. But a staff person alone cannot carry a campaign. The volunteer spirit is crucial to the successful fund drive, whether it involves direct mail, events, membership, planned gifts or personal soliciation.

Certainly, true commitment in a staff person is a great asset. But no matter how dedicated your development officer is, the words of a volunteer will be the words that really make a difference in gathering support.

- ***"I've never done this before. I'll wait till I've been on the board longer."***

Training really makes a difference. Longevity does not. Try to bring some experienced, volunteer fundraisers to your meetings to talk about their own learning process. For solicitation, try role play; people say they hate it, but practicing really does make asking easier.

It's also important to note that fundraising has many faces. The person who can run a complex direct mail campaign without a hitch may panic in a prospect's living room. The special events chairman who will happily spend three months double-checking every detail of a benefit dinner may lose patience after five minutes at the annual fund strategy meeting. Learn your volunteers' strengths and ask them to do the jobs they like and do best.

If you have the time to serve on the board, you must have the time to help raise money.

Everyone enjoys success; if you assign tasks well you will all enjoy the double success of a goal met on time. There are many jobs to be done in an annual fund drive, and if everyone helps, it gets done. No one is exempt, but diversity will push you toward your goal.

- ***"What we really need to do is get some grants. That's where the money is!"***

Grants are a wonderful source of funding for new projects, one-time expenses, experiments and other unusual expenses. While you may be lucky enough to have a foundation or two that supports you with annual gifts because of personal or geographic connections — and you should protect that funding — there is little chance that research and grant proposal writing will bring in annual funding or any money for operations on a regular basis. Continuing support of a new organization is simply not within the interests or guidelines of most foundations.

When you have a new project, go after grants to fund it. It's the perfect way to encourage experimentation within a stable organization, and to do so without denting the budget. But be aware that the project, if successful, may eventually become part of your regular operations and your annual budget. When it reaches that point of regularity, it loses its attractiveness to a foundation.

Such grants not only do not fund annual budgets, but also they often prepare you for increasing your operating budget to include the costs of the new project. Think carefully about the implications when you choose the grant-writing route.

- ***"I don't have time."***

Serving on a board takes time, and no one has limitless time. Each person must make hard personal choices about the number and type of boards to serve on. Agreeing to serve means agreeing to uphold the two basic responsibilities of the board: to develop appropriate policy and to assure financial stability. To do these two things, one must give time, thought and money.

Helping in various ways to raise money for the organization is part of the job of a board member. If you have the time to serve on the board, you must have the time to help raise money. If you don't have time, you probably should decline the invitation.

Staff and current board members must exercise real control in inviting new board members to join. If an attractive potential board member, who seems perfect for your organization, tells you that other commitments would prevent full involvement, it would be irresponsible to pressure the prospect to join the board. Find out when other commitments may decline, and ask if you can return then to invite the prospect again. But if you make deals with a prospective board member, you not only will have one fundraising exemption, but you'll have a whole board full of people asking for equal treatment.

Good fundraising is not only money coming in, it is good insurance and good public relations.

- ***"We should raise our fees and earn the money."***

Hopefully, you considered your fees carefully when you developed the budget. If the fees, admission charges or other sources of earned income are inappropriate, they should be adjusted. Just because you are a nonprofit, you do not have to operate foolishly or give away the things people can and will pay for.

But being a nonprofit also means that you are in the business of service. You cannot and will not charge fees that put your services out of the reach of your public.

Assuming you have considered the fees carefully, raising them to make fundraising unnecessary is inappropriate. As a nonprofit, there is likely always to be a gap between income and expense. There is, also, likely always to be an annual fund. You need to face up to this and take action, not avoidance.

- ***"There are just too many important things this board needs to work on, to spend our time fundraising."***

Ask yourselves to make a list of more important things. Compare them to the value of a stable budget, consistent income and the tremendous asset of planning time that you will gain when fundraising is not a crisis situation. Then it should be clear that routine annual fundraising, tackled regularly, effectively and intelligently, will keep your organization operating at its best, as much as any other part of the board's work.

When your budget is balanced through good fundraising, you have the time to consider all your operations, you have the ability to attract the finest staff people, you have the ability to attract the best board members, and you have enormous skills to draw on if other income falters. Good fundraising is not only money coming in, it is good insurance and good public relations.

- ***"We'd be better off with the finance committee handling fundraising."***

Finally, there is this avoidance technique cloaked in the guise of efficiency. This is the combination finance/fundraising committee.

Every good board member wants to avoid too many committees and duplicated work, which is good sense. But the board member who wants also to avoid fundraising can do so by advocating a lower budget at the finance committee meetings. Lean budgets are admirable, but slashing budgets to avoid inevitable fundraising is not. As long as the fundraising/finance committee can eliminate expense rather than bring in more money, the program stands to lose. Too modest a budget can decimate a program. Ignoring the need for careful growth can force an organization to decline. In the interests of checks and balances, have one committee decide how much money is needed, and another decide how to raise it.

18 WHEN TO HIRE HELP

As you have probably discovered, there are hundreds of individual consultants and consulting firms that offer their services to nonprofits. Some are excellent, some are not. If you decide to hire one, you will have to make careful choices in selecting a consultant, but first you need to examine the circumstances that have brought you to the point of hiring an outsider.

There are a few very good reasons to hire outside help:

- to help you understand your organization's needs and problems
- to give you fresh perspective
- to find new solutions to problems
- to teach you new ways to do things
- to fill gaps in your skills
- to complete an essential assignment when you are out of time
- to explore the need for adding staff later.

Basically, if you have done all you can, and the job simply doesn't get finished or doesn't get done right, you may need a consultant. You probably would be better off, in the long run, if you hire someone who can show you ways to do it yourselves, than if you hire someone who will come in and tie up loose ends for you. Also, if you are stranded without the skills needed for a specific, one-time assignment, you may need a consultant.

Basically, if you have done all you can, and the job simply doesn't get finished or doesn't get done right, you may need a consultant.

The bad reasons to hire consultants are:

- You have procrastinated so long that the deadline is here and the job is undone.
- Your volunteers haven't come through and you need extra hands.
- No one else is willing to do the solicitations.

As tortuous as it might be, you might be better off in the long run admitting weaknesses in these situations, writing off your mistakes and starting to plan for a more effective fund next year. Fixing the problem in the dark, without learning how to do it right, almost guarantees you'll be back in the same spot next year.

If you hire for the right reasons, and get a good consultant, there will be some great side-effects in addition to getting the initial job done. Most of these advantages will be for your staff and volunteers' professional advancement, but don't worry about it because ultimately the organization wins. You will:

- learn new problem-solving and fundraising skills
- expand organizational capacity
- achieve challenging goals
- have an advocate with the board
- learn how to be your own consultant

Beware "commission thinking." No one giving money likes to hear that a percentage of every dollar goes to the paid solicitor.

You'll discover that consultants often work by asking questions, listening carefully to the spoken and unspoken answers, and then drawing conclusions based on their assessment of your situation and their stored experiences. Knowing this will help you in selecting a consultant, as it will give you a perspective in interviewing and judging the applicants. Use the same approach, and ask yourself how far you can advance with each potential consultant.

In the annual fund, a consultant will be useful for several phases of the operation. You'll save money in the long run using the same individual throughout because the concept will stay strong, you won't waste time informing a new consultant about your needs, and one step can mesh with the next. Some tasks you can effectively share with the consultant will be:

- assessing your needs and the effectiveness of previous campaigns
- developing the overall annual fund plan
- setting goals and deadlines
- establishing board and volunteer teams
- training your solicitors
- creating a flow system for receipts, acknowledgments and records.

Consultants are not the most effective solicitors, and in fact many will refuse such work for philosophical or ethical reasons. Many states now have fundraising legislation that limits paid nonstaff solicitation work and places severe requirements for bonding and reporting on the part of the hiring organization. But the first reason not to use a consultant for solicitation is that a paid nonstaff person is simply not able to make a convincing argument with sincerity. They can only appear as they are: paid fundraisers. That will not draw money from your prospects' pockets.

Some organizations hire outsiders to run events and benefits. While this is certainly a matter of organizational choice, it seems a waste of good money. Events and benefits are highly labor-intensive projects, and the greatest money can be raised only if administrative costs are minimal. They are also some of the best, and often only, ways to use volunteers. One of the finest characteristics distinguishing nonprofits from all other kinds of organizations is the availability and willing devotion of volunteers. Why not use that advantage?

Beware "commission thinking." Some consultants will work on commission, a very attractive idea to organizations with poor fundraising skills and history. The theory is: "We'll only have to pay on the money that comes in, and anything we get is better than nothing." That's settling for the least return on your volunteer investment and belittles your donors at the same time. No one giving money likes to hear that a percentage of every dollar goes to the paid solicitor. A good advisor will cost you money up front but the pay-offs will continue for a long time.

Commissions have been the source of much professional debate in the fundraising world. Currently, most professional associations take a stand against fundraisers working on commission. Regardless of any change in that trend, you will always be able to find consultants on either side. For the health and long-term good reputation of your organization, you are better off paying a fixed fee, or paying on a per diem basis.

Make sure, in hiring a fundraising consultant, that you find someone with the skills you need. You will be paying far more, whether per project or per diem, than you would for staff. For a finite situation, such as planning a campaign or writing direct mail letters, someone with narrow experience may be fine. However, if you need to resolve organizational problems or wide-ranging fundraising crises, you need someone who has been in the business a long time and has real depth of experience. Hold out for the right consultant for your situation; the person who helped you write winning grants last year may be entirely inadequate to help you head off a volunteer revolt.

Of course, the short-term nature of consulting contracts is one of the best things about them. Keep this in mind, and don't sign up for more help than you need. You are in control of this situation and can hire just what you need, when you need it. Develop a contract with your outside help and make sure it provides a clear end to the arrangement as well as means for early conclusion if necessary or useful.

When you hire help, be prepared to accept it — or at least to hear it! Don't hire a consultant and then defensively refuse all suggestions. There are no punishments for past inadequacies, but failing to take advantage of the consultant's offerings is a terrible waste.

Share your information. Tell what you've tried and how it worked or failed. Don't withhold; your consultant is your partner and advocate. If you are not comfortable sharing confidential material and signs of weakness with your consultant, you have hired the wrong person. It is the consultant's job to hold your information in confidence, to let you understand that and encourage your comfort in sharing those confidences.

You may logically put up a good front with others, but when you talk with your consultant you must give the total picture or you will not get the best possible advice.

It is much cheaper to hire a consultant for a short-term or finite assignment, even if the hourly or per diem rate surprises you. Consider the expense of hiring staff for a short time, including the search, benefits and office add-ons. Consider, too, the expense of laying off an unnecessary employee when the job is done. Used well, a consultant offers you a shot in the arm for a one-time price.

As valuable as it is to hire a consultant from time to time, to offer you a sense of perspective, a fresh view and new ideas and techniques, you cannot always do it. In that case, look within your organization, or to

A consultant who can prod your group into greater understanding, better planning and more determination will have a more lasting impact than one who brings you quick-fix solutions.

potential donors. Perhaps you have enough experience to deal with the organizational problems or challenges yourself — if only you could decide where to begin.

We've all heard the expression that consultants are people who borrow your watch to tell you what time it is. To an extent, that is true. The perspective an experienced outsider can bring to your group is worth a great deal. Throughout this book there are lists of criteria and questions that are the equivalent of the "watches" a consultant might borrow from you to help you make the decisions you know must be made. Use these lists to approach your annual fund planning from a consultant's point of view, and you can train yourselves to come up with intelligent plans and directions.

Despite the hope that a consultant will solve your problems, you will be better off with a consultant who can help you do the problem solving. That provides you with prevention at the same time as you make progress. A consultant who can prod your group into greater understanding, better planning and more determination will have a more lasting impact than one who brings you quick-fix solutions. Take advantage of the perspective you can gain on your own organization by asking these questions, and do not settle for easy answers.

After you've been using this book to help you plan, you may still find there would be value to getting outside help. If so, you will save time and money by using your consultant to best advantage: pushing you beyond your own limitations and expanding your fundraising abilities.

19 GOOD RECORDS MAKE GOOD DONORS

One of the most valuable contributions you can make to your organization is a promise for the future. You can almost ensure increasingly professional, effective fundraising by keeping excellent records. Even the smallest group needs to know its past in order to improve.

Information must be stored accessibly in your organization's files; depending on the donor's giving potential, you may also need to maintain personal information in hard files. You definitely need to keep gift information stored in a database, preferably with the capacity to produce mail merge letters and thank-yous.

We all know organizations that have one great "mastermind" who knows everyone and each giving history. The organization may seem lucky to you now, but I assure you that it will pay an exorbitant price one day for such reliance.

Don't store things in your head, as good as your memory may be. We all know organizations that have one great "mastermind" who knows everyone and each giving history. The organization may seem lucky to you now, but I assure you that it will pay an exorbitant price one day for such reliance.

Regardless of the size of your organization, some data should be stored in hard files, in addition to the simple giving data stored on computer as suggested in Chapter 20. The box on the facing page lists the most important records.

Even a small organization could simply staple together letters and clippings until it grows fat enough for a file. Larger organizations should combine computer storage with hard file storage for each significant donor prospect.

Even if you are primarily relying on your old metal file cabinet for useful personal information, set up a computer file on all donors with the information above (except letters, notes on calls and other documents). Your priority should be easy sorting for various purposes:

- alphabetizing by last name
- sorting by size of gift (in gift clubs as well as actual dollars)
- sorting by dollar amount
- sorting by donor category: board, volunteer, business, individual, foundation, etc.

- printing by zip code
- sorting by solicitor's name
- sorting by affiliation: member, alumnus, class year, last date of gift
- next planned approach (date)

With these capabilities you should be able to keep records of gift totals, do your preparatory work for mailings, inform your solicitors of their assignments and progress, segment prospects for various approaches, compare giving trends, and prepare personalized updates and thank-yous. Be sure to back up computer files frequently.

These simple suggestions will help you concentrate on the people rather than the systems and provide a personalized, attentive atmosphere for your campaign.

Figure 18: Donor Information Files

- prospect name
- address
- phone
- e-mail address
- giving history: gifts by year and by purpose (it is also useful to know the lifetime giving total and largest single gift)
- volunteer/committee association with the organization
- contacts with personnel in organization
- solicitors' names (and years)
- nicknames, spouse's and children's names
- type of donor (business, foundation, individual)
- programmatic interests
- copies of letters and notes of phone calls to and from donor
- newspaper clippings on the donor and family (especially obituaries)
- comments made by solicitors after seeing the donor
- call reports
- written explanation of the family relationships
- copies of any solicitation strategy plans

20 TOOLS OF THE TRADE

When it comes to equipment, fundraising is very much like cooking. There are many sophisticated tools available which will speed your work, allow you to do some fancy things, and help you to make a beautiful presentation, but you can actually achieve wonderful results with the most basic materials.

Perhaps you will be able to buy sophisticated computer equipment and fundraising software, purchase mailing lists, print four-color brochures and accummulate an impressive library of fundraising literature. But perhaps your budget won't allow it. There is no need to go overboard, and you should make every effort to keep your supplies, publications and equipment budget modest and appropriate to your goal. If you are running a relatively small annual campaign (particularly under $100,000) your donors do not need to see a glossy colorful case statement. In fact, a slick production may turn off your prospective donors and interfere with your effectiveness in fundraising.

> ***There is no need to go overboard, and you should make every effort to keep your supplies, publications and equipment budget modest and appropriate to your goal.***

On the other hand, if you have a development staff (not just one person, or one of you desperately combining fundraising with other tasks), it would probably be foolish not to accummulate fundraising texts and resource books because that would be cheaper in the long run than time spent traveling, copying and borrowing information. The costs of these tools will seem small in comparison to your overall goals.

In building a strong development operation and a reasonable annual budget for fundraising, one of your primary assignments will be to ascertain the appropriate level of expense for fundraising tools.

Not all your development tools are purchased from the outside. The most important ones are those you produce yourself: everything from a one-page photocopied fact sheet to a four-color magazine. Cost is not the only factor in developing those tools. The image you make, both in regard to your mission and in regard to your cost-effectiveness, will be crucial to your efforts.

PUBLICATIONS

Every fundraising effort relies to some extent on the printed word. Even a fancy benefit dinner needs a printed invitation that lives up to the anticipatory image of the event. The types of publications that you need may range from a case statement, a basic mission-related brochure or a newsletter, to a magazine or an occasional book. When you begin to plan publications, understand your audience. Ask yourselves:

- What type of people will read this?
- Are we satisfied with the type of donors we have now, or are we reaching out to a new audience?
- What are the readers looking for?
- Do we have competition to worry about?
- What is their image?
- Will it help to look "low-budget" or not?

We typically think of case statements as part of a capital campaign, but a modest case can be very useful in an annual appeal. The "case" is a printed document that expresses your need for funds to achieve a particular goal. Even a very brief statement that expresses mission and goals, the budget, sources of income and the goal for the annual campaign, helps you describe to your prospective donor precisely what his or her money will be used for.

Preparation of the case statement is an important exercise which should be shared by your fundraising committee and your staff because it allows you to thrash out the difficult points among yourselves instead of among your prospects. It assures you that the same argument for support will be given to all of your prospects.

You may find it particularly effective to print a very small annual fund summary that can be inserted in your organization's brochure. That way, the issue of money and fundraising can be added to or deleted from the basic brochure as need be, and you can hand somebody a very specific statement on fundraising needs when you want to be brief. This is also a good idea because you can develop a mission brochure which can be used for several years without change, incorporating the economies of scale that may allow you to print a fancier brochure, and you can insert an annually revised annual fund description with budget and goal. With the advent of desk-top publishing, you can accomplish much more sophisticated design at far lower cost than we would have imagined ten years ago. Even without computer equipment or knowledge, you can work with a designer whose work cuts out middle steps such as typesetting and layout. You'll save money and enormous amounts of time.

A graphic artist can help you develop a fancy case statement, but a good clean simple flyer may do the trick. If your budget is tight, or if you are fundraising for a small amount, try making a neatly typed single-sheet description of your annual appeal, perhaps with an abbreviated budget printed on the back side. Copies made at your local quick-print place (or even photocopied on your office machine) may be all you need. If not, your typed version gives you a good starting point with a designer and guarantees clarity and directness.

Remember to be creative about paying for publications. Since these are some of the few truly tangible aspects of fundraising, they lend themselves to in-kind giving. With the promise of credits on the flyer itself, you may be able to attract reduced rates and donations from the designer, the print house, the distribution company (if you use one) or even the writer or marketer who helps you design it.

If those direct ideas fail, consider asking business to make an annual contribution toward the cost of any or all of your publications, again with printed credit on the documents. Just don't compromise or allow an ineffective product to suit the donors' publicity needs. For instance, while a slick four-color flyer might demonstrate the generosity of your donor, it might be giving the wrong message to other supporters of your grass-roots organization who want to see maximum dollars in program. The fact that your donor will only give for publications simply is not a good argument.

Brochures

Almost any organization can benefit from a brochure describing its work, to be used in fundraising. Once again, you must determine the style and sophistication of your brochure, the colors, the type of paper, and the length that will carry the right message to your members and prospects. The text itself should focus on the basic mission of the organization, so any emissary may be able to use the brochure as assistance in describing your reason for being.

A brochure is more effective if it has some pictures in it. Quotations from your clients, audience or members can make far more impact than verbiage. In creating a brochure, put yourself in the place of the reader, and imagine that you have 20 to 30 seconds (your real reader may not spend that long!) to look over the brochure. Board members, staff and close friends may spend longer with the flyer, but they are not the ones you are trying to attract! It's very important that the brochure grabs attention with visual impact from the start.

In most cases, it is best to develop a brochure that is not dated. You should be able to order them in quantity and have your supply last for some time so that reprinting your brochure is not a recurring expense. If some aspects of your organization are in immediate transition, postpone printing the brochure for a short time so things can sort out. If change seems inevitable but you must print now, print a smaller number but use a format that can be adapted inexpensively.

Almost any organization can benefit from a brochure describing its work, to be used in fundraising.

It seems that old brochures stay in people's hands and on their desks for a very long time after the information contained has gone out of date, just like return gift envelopes with the wrong address, or phone books with old phone numbers.

If your offices have public areas such as reception rooms, foyers, lobbies, or frequented offices, leave a supply of your brochures available to the public. For one thing, people then can get the answers to their questions without feeling nosy about your organization. For another thing, you can never be quite sure where your new donors will come from, and someone who is spending time at your facility may take a liking to you and wonder where to send money! Or they may pass the brochure on to a family member or friend who is interested. People like to feel self-sufficient about figuring out such things, so you can be quietly helpful via the printed word.

Newsletters

A newsletter can help you explain your current activities, describe your plans for the future, encourage your readers to be sympathetic to your cause, and ask for continuing contributions, all in a friendly, but impersonal way.

A newsletter is not the answer for everyone, but for those who can benefit from widespread communication, the newsletter is one of the best creations of the 20th century. Computerization has made communication by newsletters remarkably simple, and even if you do not have in-house graphics capability, there are many small businesses that can help you out very cheaply.

Some people bemoan the "information age" and are distressed to receive so much junk mail and paper. Certainly your members and donors will feel the same way. However, regardless of our impatience with throw-aways, we have come to expect a very high level of information sharing and communication. No one is content any longer to sit back and let a nonprofit go about its business, particularly when the reader is a donor, without knowing what that business is. A newsletter can help you explain your current activities, describe your plans for the future, encourage your readers to be sympathetic to your cause, and ask for continuing contributions, all in a friendly, but impersonal way. If your organization resists frequent, even monthly, direct mail solicitations, you can use a newsletter as a way of reminding donors that you are alive and well, and needing funds.

A newsletter does not need to be monthly, nor slick, nor graphically sophisticated, nor academic. It need not be written by a professional. It does need to be basically literate, interesting, timely, and clean cut. Your newsletter should have an editorial policy and it should promote you in the way you choose to be promoted. It should be reliable: if you promise it three times a year, make sure it reaches your readers three times a year. If you can't guarantee that, call it an "occasional" publication and everyone will be satisfied.

Magazines

If you are a fairly large organization, or if you are part of a national organization, or if your mission is best expressed visually, a magazine may be a worthwhile way for you to spend your money. A magazine is also increasingly important if you have a large number of members who have no other form of communication, or who are deeply interested in each other's activities.

A magazine can be a major expense, and it can devour staff time with editorial and graphic demands. But you need not let the magazine become a tyrant in your operation; remember it is the tool of your organization, not the mission. Like a newsletter, it can be published on any schedule you choose so long as you stick to your schedule. If you are short of staff time, short of staff writers, or short of money, a magazine may not be the most appropriate form of communication for your organization. However, if your experience with your members has proven that they communicate best through the printed word, you may find that a magazine is an important way for you to garner support.

Occasional Publications

If you are on the fence about publishing a magazine, yet sense that

Publications can expand to consume all the available time (and even some unavailable time) of all of the people in an organization if you are not careful.

your members and donors would respond well to one, you might try a single publication. You could issue an annual report which includes interesting articles about organizational activities or members' work. One of the advantages of an occasional publication is that it attracts attention from members and donors, and they will probably read it carefully, simply because they have seen nothing else like it from you in the past. This is all the more reason to make sure it is attractive, literate, and fulfills a need.

Other occasional publications might be collections of study papers, research reports, publication of literary or artistic work, collections of case studies exploring the work done by your agency, or historical documents. These books or booklets can be highly effective communication tools with donors and members, and can also be an excellent way to reach out to the public. Because they are usually one-time efforts, you may be able to obtain grant support for their production.

Do not embark casually on a publications project. Do not assign it to a board committee and expect everyone else to love the final product a year later. When an organization produces a long-lasting publication, there should be enough editorial control to assure a high-quality production that represents the organization well. Treat the production of the book like a business operation, taking bids, examining the work of several writers or designers, and investigating carefully all the marketing and distribution avenues.

Publications can expand to consume all the available time (and even some unavailable time) of all of the people in an organization if you are not careful; you must not allow them to overwhelm your basic services. However, the right print material can be a marvelous opportunity for an organization to expand its reach, document its past, and improve its overall image.

When you consider publications, ask yourself these questions:

- Who will read this publication?
- Is this a publication for people who already know us and like us, or is it meant to find us new supporters?
- Why do we want this publication?
- Are we trying to change our image, or do we need to reinforce our current mission?
- What do the readers need to know?
- How are we surviving without it so far?
- How many copies would we need?
- Who will write it and who will design it?
- How much will it cost?
- How will we distribute it?
- Is there a cheaper and more efficient way to communicate?
- Will it generate money by itself?
- Will it be an effective fundraising tool?

When you are developing your budget for a publication of any sort, be sure to include all the following: editorial time, graphic design, staff time, printing expense, distribution and marketing expense, postage, storage, printing costs, promotional costs and advertising. Include, to the best of your ability, staff time that will indirectly be applied to the publication, from the planning stages right through to distribution and even inventory control.

You may be able to garner income to support your publication. Consider earning income to pay the costs:

- restricted donations
- paid subscriptions
- advertising income
- fundraising sales
- grants

You do not necessarily have to balance your income and expense on a publication if you have made a serious decision to publish in order to accomplish some other goal. But if you anticipate expense surpassing income, you and your board should carefully weigh the advantages to the organization in comparison to the financial loss you will be underwriting.

This may be a hard discussion to have, but it is much better to go into a project knowing that it will lose money and that you have decided to go ahead with it despite the loss because it has other value to you. It will also set you out immediately looking for creative funding, rather than surprising you too late in the process. The alternative to a decision early in the game is a great deal of disappointment and bickering among board members when the publication fails to live up to their expectations. Always be perfectly clear about your reasons for publishing.

COMPUTERIZATION

There is no question about the need for fundraising software in a nonprofit organization. Even the smallest group can benefit from it. Just as your computer saves you time and frustration, software will allow you to stay in touch with donors, thank them appropriately, remember what they have done and want to do for your organization, and keep track of their relationships in the organization. Your software is the key to identifying those donors who can give more, and to asking in a timely fashion.

A simple database can be used to keep basic records if you do not have a full-time position for record keeping, even if it was not designed for fundraising. Consider the possibility of using an existing database to store names, addresses, gifts, past giving, contact names, and other routine data that can be supported by a fat file of notes and clippings. If you are careful to store your information in a form that allows easy sorting and merging for your in-office purposes, you can survive for a long time with such a system.

However, you can also purchase fundraising software that will hold all your records of donors, gifts, prospects, volunteer assignments, projections and campaign progress, and that will file, sort, integrate and separate them all. Do you really need that? Or, if you know you need it, are you able to make use of all that information to augment fundraising?

If you don't need it right now, do you anticipate growing into the need?

To decide about software and the major move to computerizing your fundraising, you should ask yourselves:

- What tasks need to be done?
- Can we make use of the added information and capability?
- Is our work this complex already, or is something happening to make it more complex?
- Do we have the staff time to manage the software and its products, such as reports, reminders, and correspondence?
- Can our current computers handle this, or will it require new hardware?

Fundraising software needs an informed operator to make it work at full capacity. You'll need good support inside and outside the office to make it work for you, rather than you working for it. If you relay on many volunteers to stop in, help out, and pass their work on to the next volunteer, you must be prepared for a lot of education time, possibly on a continuing basis. The possibility of error and loss with volunteers unfamiliar with programs is enormous. Also, confidentiality may be threatened with volunteers helping.

Buying software is not like buying a new pair of shoes. It is not even like buying a new car: it's like buying a school bus. You are about to place your most valuable information, and your most sensitive data, in a machine. You must be able to get it out again, at will, in the condition you need.

Remember the adage "Buyer beware." All the ads say the software works miracles. Like soap, not all programs are as miraculous as their promotions. You can ensure a good choice if you take your time, investigate, and experiment. If you are serious about computerizing, be a cautious buyer:

- Shop through publishers, consultant firms, and suppliers that specialize in nonprofits, not just your local computer store.
- Do not choose simply on the basis of price, either high *or* low!
- Make sure the program was designed by, or in partnership with, a reputable fundraiser with broad experience.
- Make a list of your needs before you start shopping.
- Ask other nonprofits in your field for recommendations.
- Imagine what you may need in two to five years, given growth or planned changes.
- If at all possible, find out if the software company has plans to move, merge, or otherwise change its administration.

When you make your choice, then:

- Find out all the hardware you'll need, including utility lines and extra phones or lines.
- Make certain continuing support is included, and at what cost.
- Talk to another fundraising organization that has used the software you are considering.
- Use the software yourselves on a sample disk.
- Involve your staff in the decision.
- Find out how long it will take to install and get working.
- Determine how long it will take, and who will be qualified, to transfer all your current data into the new software.
- Keep backups of your old system, and maintain your hard files with care.

As this list might indicate, this is not a simple decision. This is not like buying a new pair of shoes. It is not even like buying a new car: it's like buying a school bus. You are about to place your most valuable information, and your most sensitive data, in a machine. You must be able to get it out again, at will, in the condition you need. You must be certain that it will not be garbled or lost and that it will do what you need most: act fast and efficiently. You also probably want to make certain your existing staff can use it.

If you are thinking of fundraising software because things are not going as well as planned in your fundraising efforts, stop right there. The time to implement new software is when things are going well.

Early in the days of fundraising software, many organizations hired a computer programmer to custom-design their own program. While that may have worked for some, it usually ended up with too many glitches, too many cumbersome commands for in-office staff, and too much time in the making. Support was often gone when something went wrong, and other people could not easily step in to fix or adapt it. In the long run, it was probably not cheaper.

Having your own person design the software is a wasteful reinvention of the wheel. If you do not find the perfect software in your search, keep searching. Ask fundraisers what they recommend, and consult with any network or association that is affiliated with your operation.

One last word. Remember that software and computers will not make you better fundraisers than you already are. They do not work miracles. Computers do not solicit donors! Software can only manipulate the data you already have. It can speed things up, make you more efficient, and help you make yourselves more effective. Best of all, it frees you to do more personal solicitation.

If you are thinking of fundraising software because things are not going as well as planned in your fundraising efforts, stop right there. The time to implement new software is when things are going well, and when you have a strong plan and know you will be getting ready for new efforts, like campaigns. Then the software will be there to help you manage.

CONTINUING EDUCATION

The basics of fundraising do not really change. This is not a technological field that encourages obsolescence. However, there is lots of room for improvement, creativity, and broadened scope, and you will benefit enormously from personal and organizational education. Besides the advantage of learning new things, most continuing education in the fundraising field will bring you in contact with others who do the same work, and you can help each other with ideas and problem solving.

Fundraising, even in the most secure and endowed organizations, is stressful work. People, causes, workers, and communities depend on us to keep the machines oiled, and the pressure is constant. It will help you to talk to others who do this work and gain from their experience, as they will from yours. Obviously, you do not give away your donors and hot prospects, but you can share equally valuable advice with each other.

Workshops and Seminars

This must be the age of the training seminar. Everywhere, you will

Look for a program that will allow questions, answers, participant discussion and some flexibility.

find people and businesses offering short-term training programs, workshops, presentations, seminars, brown-bag lunches and more. Some will, of course, be time-wasters for you, but with care you can select one or two that will expand your abilities or understanding dramatically. Try the smaller ones first, because you'll be able to deal with issues most relevant to your organization and, with luck, ask specific questions.

If you are trying to educate yourself or a staff person about a new area, such as planned giving, be sure to determine whether the program is offered for beginners or experts. Find out what other organizations are sending participants, as that will help you decide if the discussions will be useful for you.

Before you enroll, ask for a copy of the agenda for the program and the credentials of the presenter. Look for items that you are really curious about and for a presenter who has worked with organizations like your own. For instance, someone with a career in national health nonprofits will probably be less helpful for a small town arts council than either an arts consultant or a community consultant. Look for a program that will allow questions, answers, participant discussion and some flexibility.

If you happen to work for a smaller, local affiliate of a regional or national organization, venture out. You'll probably be expected to attend training programs scheduled by your own headquarters, but those may be consistently taught by in-house people. You can learn a great deal from sharing, but the information can be limited. You'll find less bias, and more diversity in ideas, when you attend public seminars.

Don't spend your entire training budget on one seminar. You need variety, you need to explore the options, and you need to get out and meet people in your field. Once is not enough. Also, do not reserve these experiences for the novices on your staff. The old-timers need refreshment as well as education.

Conferences

If there are no reasonably priced, interesting conferences offered in your area, set one up yourself.

Conferences are also wonderful for sharing information. Of course you cannot spend your work life on the road, but do try to attend some programs on topics relevant to your work, or with representatives of other similar organizations.

Nearly every field has professional associations, and your contacts there may prove very useful and educational. Join the association and meet your peers. The National Association of Fund Raising Executives (NSFRE) may have a chapter near you, and that can be an excellent way to stay in touch with other fundraisers and learn what the state of the art really is.

One of the worst things about fundraising and small nonprofits is isolation from other professionals. It is demoralizing to face the same frustrations daily without anyone to talk with, and at conferences you can spill out those problems and hear some creative solutions, or at least a voice of understanding. Some days you'll even discover that, despite your own uncertainties, you are able to help someone else.

If there are no reasonably priced, interesting conferences offered in your area, set one up yourself. If there is no chance for fundraisers to talk together, invite a group to gather informally for lunch, late afternoon, or breakfast in a central place, and suggest a topic. You can survive as a healthy group for a long time simply by scheduling a short presentation by a member at the beginning of each meeting. You might eventually present a larger conference on fundraising topics using your own skills. Whatever you do, get together and talk. It really helps.

NETWORKING

A donor you might have no luck with, who does not share your goals, might be very happy to give the local library a grant to purchase development resources that could be used by all local nonprofits.

Networking is the 80's invention for comraderie, talk, help, and sharing. With increasing pressure on schedules, it becomes harder to share in a natural way, and this new verb arrived to give credibility to an age-old habit. Whatever you call it, it is very good for you and for your organization.

Much of networking refers to personal advancement: finding connections and making the most of them to pursue career changes. This cannot be ignored, since the development and fundraising fields are high on the list for short-term jobs, frequent moves and personal opportunity. (The average development professional stays at a job for two years.) This amount of mobility is not healthy for the organizations, though, and more continuity in fundraising would be a great advantage to the nonprofits. There are also ways to use networking to advance one's skills and contacts, and for professional gratification, without having to move so often.

One way organizations can use networking to advantage is in seeking new staff. With good connections, you can find capable, promising staff far faster and more reliably than by placing ads in papers. If you need to hire someone, be sure to call around and ask those in the field whom they know. Check references this way too. You'll get your most straightforward advice from your friends in the field.

LIBRARIES

Development offices, small and large, have a tendency to isolate themselves from the rest of the world. In fact, they are often isolated from the very organization they raise money for. Perhaps because of overwork or sensitive information, there's a belief that we've got all the information we can deal with, and if it's not here, in the office, we don't need it.

The fact is, there's lots of information out there that would make a big difference for you, but you probably can't afford it all and you can't take the time to select it.

This is not a new problem. This is the reason why libraries were invented! Think about your library, internal or community, and the ways you could use it better. For the small organization, the local library can become a major asset. All the books of data that you cannot afford, and that your peer organizations cannot afford, could be purchased by the library and shared. A donor you might have no luck with, who does not share your goals, might be very happy to give the local library a grant to purchase development resources that could be used by all local nonprofits.

If you think this is a poor idea because the library doesn't have the right books, get involved in the selection. You might also consider getting a group of nonprofits to make a contribution to the library to assist in purchase of several important data books and papers, such as foundation directories, corporate giving listings, and the *Chronicle of Philanthropy*, plus regional funding publications. If that idea doesn't catch on, try applying to a local foundation to fund development support books in the library. It's a great way for a small local group to give to many organizations at once.

Don't miss out on the periodicals you can subscribe to in this way also. The variety of professional journals, newsletters and easy-reading newspapers and magazines for fundraisers is fabulous. There are also series of research journals reporting on trends, needs and studies of nonprofits. It would be nice to get all of them, and skim when you have the time, but it's hard to justify that for a small shop. The library is the perfect place for these.

In selecting books for your own library or the public library, save the many "junk" mail promotions you receive for fundraising books and clip reviews that appear in funding journals. Then sit down occasionally and review the whole list, trying to achieve some diversity and excellence with your purchase. Don't order haphazardly, just because a book promotion comes along with good graphics or a low price. Ask around and find out who the best authors are, with the greatest experience, and which books have helped others. See the reading list at the end of this book for some focused suggestions.

Two other advantages of libraries: if you are concerned about not using up the world's resources, as all of us should be, and to which many nonprofits are publicly committed, the library is a better storage place for publications. There is less waste if the product is shared.

Also, if stress and demand on your attention is making you miserable, you probably need some quiet time in your work day. An hour at the library, catching up with progress in the field, without a phone and interruptions, may have benefits in personal peace and organizational efficiency that far surpass the most enlightening articles you read.

21 COMPETITION, COOPERATION AND COLLABORATION

Consider the advantages of hooking up with your related competitor: sharing staff, space, overhead, boards, committees, you name it. Could your overlapping functions be run more economically by one organization?

Fundraising has never been easy, and lately it has gotten even tougher.

Fundraising has never been easy, and lately it has gotten even tougher. The main reason is the increasing competition. Despite our hopes that we rise above marketing scrambles, back-biting campaigns and manipulative public relations, there is a natural tendency to want to "beat out" the competition.

However, when you are asking for donations on the basis of goodwill, good works and kindness of spirit, competition is an anomaly. One of the challenges for nonprofits today is to strive for maximum fundraising within a tolerance, if not encouragement, of diverse and similar causes. Our society needs a wide variety of nonprofit efforts and solutions to problems. There is no single way to improve life, nor is there any way to create a solution that all donors will embrace.

If your organization competes aggressively against another nonprofit to tackle the same societal problems, you have a fascinating situation on your hands. Do you increase your efforts to garner gifts at any cost? Vary your programs, add extra mailings, schedule special events close to those of your competitor? Hire away their development people, woo their board members, imitate their successes? Second guess their new approaches?

All this supplanting of efforts takes enormous staff energy and time. That same time spent developing a highly distinctive voice and message for your organization might be equally, or more, successful. It would certainly be more ethical. If we are in the business of "doing good," why stay awake nights worrying that someone else may be doing better? But take another look. Even though some of us are rooted in long-established friendly (or not-so-friendly) sparring matches, cooperation may be the most effective solution of all. Times are not getting easier. Consider the advantages of hooking up with your related competitor: sharing staff, space, overhead, boards, committees, you name it. Could your overlapping functions be run more economically by one organization?

If that thought is too much to bear, or too much too soon, consider other possibilities. For example, you might:

- meet with competing groups and divide the target problems into more manageable pieces that will keep each mission focused and tight
- share space, equipment or overhead with related, nonduplicative organizations
- jointly purchase major equipment and work out cooperative use arrangements (for vans, desktop publishing, specialized health equipment)
- develop shared employee benefit plans that will result in lower costs for each group
- cooperate on one or two intense, large fundraising events rather than struggling to do two smaller ones each
- approach local government together with mutual agreement in search for town/regional funding
- engage training consultants together, and participate in joint seminars
- encourage local networking to share information and help each other in problem solving
- establish networking groups regionally for staff and for board to talk, explore problems and solutions, and to educate each other.

At first glance, these do not seem suggestions directly related to annual fundraising. But remember, you only have to raise enough money to meet your budget. If you can save money, and still accomplish your goals, your fundraising needs may go down. Your volunteers may feel less daunted. Your staff may have more time to spend directly on fulfillment of the mission.

Do promote cost-effectiveness with your organization, streamlining, and tight control. Do promote great care in budgeting, and understand that smaller budgets require less annual fundraising. But also be courageous and innovative in cost-saving. If you can network, cooperate, and combine human and technical resources with other groups, you may be able to lower your operating budget and achieve consistently higher goals.

Your donors and prospects will be impressed with your ability to cross over to other organizations in a cooperative spirit. Your efficiency and effectiveness will gain you as many admirers as do your programmatic achievements.

Any prospect you approach who has business experience will assess your operations with a business eye. Most people think of the nonprofit sector as the human, and humane, sector, where cause supplants ego and individual goals exist primarily to promote mission. We may not be ready to live up to all those lofty attributes, but we can begin with cooperation that serves all participants.

READING LIST

On Gift Solicitation

Asking and *Practice Makes Perfect,* two booklets to build gift solicitation skills, by Christine Graham. CPG Enterprises, P.O. Box 199, Shaftsbury, VT 05262.

On Basic Fundraising

Confessions of a Fund Raiser by Maurice G. Gurin. Order from the Association of Fundraising Professionals (AFP), previously known as the National Society of Fund Raising Executives (NSFRE), (800) 666-3863; www.nsfre.org or www.afp.org.

Discover Total Resources: A Guide for Nonprofits. Published by the Mellon Bank Corporation. Available free to nonprofits from the Mellon Bank, (412) 234-3275.

Fundraising for the Long Haul and *Fundraising for Social Change* by Kim Klein. Chardon Press, 3781 Broadway, Oakland, CA 94611, (888) 458-8588 or fax (510) 596-8822; www.chardonpress.com.

The Grass Roots Fundraising Book: How to Raise Money in Your Community and *Successful Fundraising* by Joan Flanagan. Order from the Association of Fundraising Professionals (AFP), previously known as the National Society of Fund Raising Executives (NSFRE), (800) 666-3863; www.nsfre.org or www.afp.org.

On Major Gift Fundraising

The Artful Journey by William T. Sturtevant. Bonus Books, 160 East Illinois Street, Chicago, IL 60611.

The Seven Faces of Philanthropy by R. A. Prince and K. M. File. Jossey-Bass Inc. Publishers, 350 Sansome Street, San Francisco, CA 94104.

On Planned Giving

The Art of Planned Giving by Douglas E. White. Published by John Wiley and Sons (1997). Order from Jossey-Bass Inc., Publishers, 350 Sansome Street, San Francisco, CA 94104.

On Special Event Fundraising

Organizing Special Events and Conferences: A Practical Guide for Busy Volunteers and Staff (Revised Edition) by Darcy Campion Devney. Pineapple Press, P.O. Box 3889, Sarasota, FL 34230.

On Capital Campaign Fundraising

Blueprint for a Capital Campaign by Christine Graham. CPG Enterprises, P.O. Box 199, Shaftsbury, VT 05262.

Capital Campaigns: Strategies That Work by Andrea Kihlstedt and Robert Pierpont. Aspen Publishers, (800) 638-8437.

On Board Operations

The Board Member's Book by Brian O'Connell. The Foundation Center, 79 Fifth Avenue, New York, NY 10003.

The Board Member's Guide to Fundraising by Fisher Howe. Jossey-Bass Inc., Publishers, 350 Sansome Street, San Francisco, CA 94104.

Boards That Make a Difference by John Carver. Jossey-Bass Inc., Publishers, 350 Sansome Street, San Francisco, CA 94104.

On Strategic Planning for a Nonprofit

Strategic Planning Workbook for Nonprofit Organizations by Bryan W. Barry. Amherst H. Wilder Foundation, 919 Lafond Avenue, St. Paul, MN 55104.

On Marketing a Nonprofit

The Marketing Workbook for Nonprofit Organizations by Gary J. Stern. Published by the Amherst H. Wilder Foundation, Management Support Services, 919 Lafond Avenue, St. Paul, MN 55104.

On Nonprofit Bookkeeping and Finances

How to Keep a Nonprofit Organization's Books by API-JN's Nonprofit Accounting Education Committee. Ackerson Hall 300, Rutgers University, 180 University Avenue, Newark, NJ 07102.

On Hiring Consultants

Succeeding With Consultants: Self-Assessment for the Changing Nonprofit by Barbara Kibbe and Fred Setterberg. The Foundation Center, 79 Fifth Avenue, New York, NY 10003. Supported by the David and Lucille Packard Foundation.

On Forming a Nonprofit Corporation

How to Form Your Own Nonprofit Corporation by Anthony Mancuso, J D, Nolo Publications, 950 Parker Street, Berkley, CA 94710 (for California-specific regulations, request the California edition).

Understanding and Keeping Updated on Nonprofit Developments

The Chronicle of Philanthropy, the Newspaper of the Nonprofit World, published biweekly; 1255 Third Street, NW, Washington, D.C. 20037.

Grassroots Fundraising Journal. Chardon Press, 3781 Broadway, Oakland, CA 94611, (888) 458-8588 or fax (510) 596-8822; www.chardonpress.com.

Here are some other books on similar topics from Pineapple Press. For a complete catalog, write to Pineapple Press, P.O. Box 3889, Sarasota, Florida 34230-3889, or call (800) 746-3275. Or visit our website at www.pineapplepress.com.

The Business of Special Events by Harry A. Freedman and Karen Feldman. Successful nonprofit managers know that to raise money for their cause they must approach fundraising as if it were a for-profit business. This how-to covers every aspect of producing profitable special events, from sidewalk sales to glamorous galas. ISBN 1-56164-141-3 (pb)

The Club Board Members Guide by John L. Carroll. Although written with private club members in mind, the common-sense solutions offered here apply to a much broader audience, especially those who oversee the running of a nonprofit organization. Having served on many club boards, usually as president, John Carroll shows how a fine-tuned sense of "people skills," coupled with an understanding of how every organization functions, creates an atmosphere where decisions can be made for the benefit of the club and its members. Learn what to expect as a club board member: How do you communicate effectively with your members and the public? What are your legal responsibilities? How should meetings be handled? What about issues of money? ISBN 1-56164-244-4 (pb)

Games for Fundraising by William N. Czuckrey Who doesn't love a fair? The barker's cry, "Step right up, ladies and gentlemen!," the sound of hoops clattering over pegs and balls hitting their targets, the colorful booths, the mysterious fortune-tellers—all contribute to the excitement and fun of trying your luck or skill to win a prize. And it all adds up to substantial profits for the sponsoring organization. For anyone who is faced with the challenge of creating an exciting special event to raise funds with games, this book offers a selection of games sure to delight all ages, complete with step-by-step instructions. ISBN 1-56164-074-3 (pb)

Organizing Special Events and Conferences Revised Edition by Darcy C. Devney. Here is help for anyone who has to produce a public event—from a church social or school fundraiser to a national conference. This comprehensive and practical handbook is the first to reveal all the tricks and techniques of the professional event organizer. An indispensable guide for volunteers and paid staff alike, packed with step-by-step instructions, checklists, and schedules. Helpful hints and anecdotes from professionals and volunteers working at all types of organizations supplement the author's clear organization and lively presentation. Updated to include website information and e-mail addresses for dozens of fundraising associations, catalogs and directories, and publications. ISBN 0-910923-63-9 (pb)

A Primer on Nonprofit PR: If Charity Begins at Home . . . by Kathleen A. Neal. Drawing on her thirty years of experience, Kathleen Neal defines public relations and then shows how it can be used creatively and effectively for nonprofit organizations. This book is chock full of ideas and strategies for applying solid PR techniques to the nonprofit, often accompanied by personal accounts of successful (and not so successful) PR efforts described with insight and a wry sense of humor. Plan a fundraising event, deal with a crisis, defuse a tense situation, develop a relationship with the media, and all the while promote your organization, keeping its mission in the eye of the public. Let this book be your how-to manual for a successful public relations program. ISBN 1-56164-229-0 (pb)